Preface

Databases are found in all sorts of situations that we encounter in our daily lives, from booking a flight or cinema ticket to registering as a school pupil or hospital patient. The ability to design, create and use a database now appears on all ICT curricula from a very early age, and an understanding of the basic concepts will be useful to all pupils throughout their school career and beyond.

Microsoft Access is a very powerful database which can however be used without difficulty by beginners to create simple databases. Teachers of pupils in all age groups from 10 upwards will appreciate the straightforward manner in which the capabilities of Access are explained. Pupils will find they are able to create their own databases after only a few lessons.

Basic Access 2000 is suitable for whole class, group and individual teaching. It will also be extremely useful to show teachers of all subjects who are new to ICT how to use this software and it will give them the confidence to use it in class successfully.

The purpose of this accompanying teacher's book is to

- aid in lesson preparation;
- give extra information to teachers on some more advanced topics;
- supply photocopiable worksheets to reinforce what has been learned and to test understanding.

The photocopiable sheets in this book are suitable for using away from the keyboard, and answers to all the questions will be found in the back of the book. A record sheet and a Certificate of Achievement are included.

Microsoft Access 2000 is used in all the examples, but schools using a different version of Access will have little difficulty adapting to minor differences in the screenshots, toolbars and menu commands.

Copies of the sample databases used in the pupil's book are available for downloading from our web site **www.payne-gallway.co.uk/basicaccess.**

Pat Heathcote

Contents

Introduction

ICT in the curriculum

ICT is now recognised as a separate subject within the National Curriculum. Schools organise and deliver the curriculum in different ways, with ICT sometimes being delivered as a separate subject, and sometimes as part of a cross-curricular scheme. Whichever approach is taken, pupils cannot progress unless they are introduced to the capabilities of the various software packages they are expected to use. A number of lessons needs to be devoted to allowing pupils to acquire the necessary skills, before they are asked to put them into practice in a subject context across the curriculum. This series of books is designed to assist teachers in imparting these essential basic skills in a straightforward but entertaining and lively manner.

Lesson planning

Each chapter in this book is designed to accompany the corresponding chapter in **Basic Access 2000**. It provides a summary of the learning objectives of each chapter and some advice on any preparation required before the chapter is taught in a classroom. Possible pitfalls are pointed out, and extra tips given where these are likely to be useful.

Teachers may find that a single chapter takes more than one lesson, especially if time on the computer is limited. Extra tasks appropriate to a particular year group and area of the curriculum can be set so that databases can be planned away from the computer.

The worksheets

These will be invaluable both to reinforce skills already encountered, and as part of the learning process. They are constructed so that they can be completed away from the computer, and so that a minimum of marking is required on the part of the teacher. Answers to all questions are given in the back of the book.

Record sheet

Successful completion of the worksheets will provide clear evidence that topics have been mastered, and a record sheet is provided at the end of the book so that each pupil can keep a record of the worksheets completed.

Working at home

Many parents may want to purchase books in this series for their sons and daughters to use at home - or for that matter, to use themselves! Most people enjoy being 'tested' on what they have learned and the worksheets will give much satisfaction in this respect. Although Basic Access 2000, for which this is the companion text, is primarily aimed at pupils from year 5 upwards, people outside this age range — from 8 to 80 — will appreciate the straightforward, simple and effective approach to learning the ins and outs of presentations with Microsoft Access.

Chapter **1**

Introduction to Databases

Learning Objectives

- To understand that a simple database can be stored as a table with rows representing records and columns representing fields.
- To learn how to plan a database.
- To define the different data types that may be used in a database.
- To select a data type for each field in a database table.
- To name a database table and write down its structure.
- To understand the difference between editing the database structure and editing the actual data in a database.

New terms and vocabulary

Database package, table, field, row, column, record, data format, data type, Text data type, alphanumeric data, Number data type, Currency data type, Yes/No data type, AutoNumber data type, database structure, edit the data.

Resources needed

A computer loaded with Microsoft Access (preferably one for each pupil). Access 2000 is used in the screenshots but the exercises will work with earlier versions of Access.

Preparation

Photocopy Worksheets 1a and 1b. Computers are not needed for the first lesson. You may like to think of some examples of databases to discuss with the class, (for example a database of pets attending a vet's surgery, a video collection, a collection of books in a library, patients attending a doctor's surgery, athletes entering the Olympics, racing pigeons, customers of a bank or store.)

What to do

The purpose of this chapter is to introduce the pupils to the concept of databases; what they are and why they are used. Databases are complex applications and it is essential to understand what a database is and how to plan a database structure before starting work on the computer. It is important that the pupils understand the terms that will be used throughout the book. For example they must appreciate the difference between a row and a column and between a field, a record and a table. You can use the example of the Bird database given in the Pupil's book and other ideas you have prepared to discuss these terms with the whole class.

Gather suggestions for other databases from class members and let them figure out what fields need to be held in the table, and what information they would like to get out of the table.

Stress the importance of planning the database before entering the information into the computer. It will save time later if your initial design satisfies all the user requirements of the database, rather than trying to make design changes at a later date. During this planning phase the pupils will need to assign data types to the fields so use plenty of examples to ensure that they can select these appropriately. The pupils could draw out a table like Figure 1.3 as an example of a database structure. Give the table a name that follows the standard naming convention i.e. the name should start with **tbl**. They could then draw a table with field names as column headings and put some data into it.

Check that the pupils understand the difference between the database structure and the actual data that will be held in the database.

Give out the first worksheet (Sheet 1a). Extension Sheet 1b can be used as an extra activity.

Sheet 1a Introduction to Databases

(Classwork)

Name: ______________________________ **Date:** ______________

A vet keeps the following database about pets that have visited the surgery.

Pet Number	Name	Type	Date of last visit	Reason for visit	Cost of treatment
1	Moji	Cat	11/06/2000	Flu vaccine	£12.00
2	Millie	Cat	11/06/2000	Flu vaccine	£12.00
3	Rover	Dog	05/05/2000	Broken Leg	£50.00
4	Sammy	Rabbit	12/08/2000	Not eating his food	£5.00
5	Fluff	Hamster	01/07/2000	Trapped	£17.50

1. How many **records** are there in the database?

   Answer: ______________________________

2. How many **fields** are there in the database?

   Answer: ______________________________

3. What data type are the entries in the **Name** column?

   Answer: ______________________________

4. What data type are the entries in the **Cost of Treatment** column?

   Answer: ______________________________

5 What data type are the entries in the **Date of Last Visit** column?

Answer: ______________________

---

6 What data type are the entries in the **Pet Number** column?

Answer: ______________________

---

7 Suggest a name for the database table. The name should start with the letters **tbl**.

Answer: ______________________

---

8 Suggest two extra fields that it might be useful to add to the database.

Answer: (i) ______________________

(ii) ______________________

---

9 What data types would you suggest for each of the new fields you suggested?

Answer: (i) ______________________

(ii) ______________________

---

10 Which column would you search to find all animals who had not visited the surgery for more than 6 months?

Answer: ______________________

Sheet 1b Introduction to Databases

(Extension work)

Name: ______________________ **Date:** ____________

A sports shop holds a database of its products.

Product Code	Product description	Make	Price	Quantity in stock
SL15724	Tennis racquet	Slazenger	£150.00	5
DP9765	Pack of 6 golf balls	Dunlop	£16.00	10
AD222	Scooter	Adidas	£135.00	6
AD6473	Football	Adidas	£30.00	4

1. How many **records** are there in the database?

   Answer: ______________________

2. How many **fields** are there in the database?

   Answer: ______________________

3. What data type are the entries in the **Product code** column?

   Answer: ______________________

4. What data type are the entries in the **Price** column?

   Answer: ______________________

5 What data type are the entries in the **Quantity in Stock** column?

Answer: ______________________________

6 What data type are the entries in the **Make** column?

Answer: ______________________________

7 Suggest a name for the database table. The name should start with the letters **tbl**.

Answer: ______________________________

8 Suggest two extra fields that it might be useful to add to the database.

Answer: (i) ________________________

(ii) ________________________

9 What data types would you suggest for each of the new fields you suggested?

Answer: (i) ________________________

(ii) ________________________

10 Three of the field names do not follow the recommended rule for names (they should not contain spaces). Change the field names so that they obey this rule.

Answer: ____

Chapter **2**

Creating a New Database

Learning Objectives

- To load Access and open a new, blank database.
- To name the common Access database objects; table, query, form and report.
- To recognise the Database window.
- To create a new table in Design view.
- To enter field names and corresponding data types.
- To understand the term Primary Key and define a field as the primary key.
- To save the table structure.
- To edit the table structure.

New terms and vocabulary

Database window, object, query, form, report, database window, Design View, primary key, key field.

Preparation

Find out from your network administrator if usernames and passwords are required to access the computers and, if so, what they are. Make sure that the students know where to save their work.

Go through the chapter and check any differences between the screenshots and what appears in your version of Access. There are minor differences between, for example, Access 97 and Access 2000.

Photocopy Sheet 2a, Sheet 2b (Extension work) for each pupil. The worksheets can be completed away from the computer.

What to do

You will need to explain to the class the concept of a primary key – the field which uniquely identifies each row in a database table. Before starting on the practical work it would be a good idea to think of several different ideas for database tables (birds, monarchs, videos, library books etc. and discuss what fields each table should have and what field should be the primary key. A numeric field is usually best, even if it is just 'BirdNumber', 'VideoNumber' etc. Monarchs have unique names so 'Name' e.g. **Charles II** would be a suitable key.

When entering a new table structure (see Figure 2.6 of Pupil's book) the **Description** field does not have to be entered but it can act as a useful reminder of what the field contains – for example **ContactNumber** is used for parent's telephone number so that could be put in the Description field.

Fields with a Number data type may be Long Integer, Integer, Byte, Single, Double etc. Make sure pupils understand that an integer is a whole number. A long integer data type can hold a very large number (several million). Fields defined as single or double can hold numbers with decimal points. For the purposes of this book the default type of Long Integer is fine for any field holding a whole number.

Make sure you have identified the row selector to the left of each row's field name. Practise dragging rows to move them.

Give out the first worksheet (Sheet 2a). Sheet 2b (Extension work) can be used as an extra activity.

Sheet 2a Creating a New Database

(Classwork)

Name: ______________________________ **Date:** ______________

Look at the screenshot below. It shows the structure of a table about sports events in the Olympic Games.

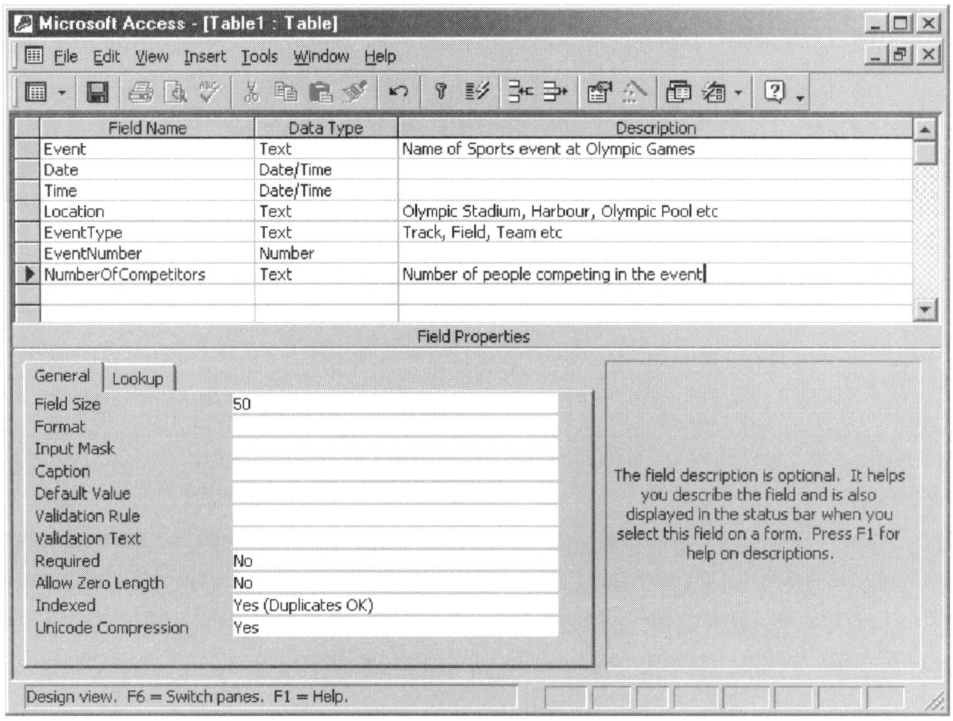

1. Suggest a name for the table that follows the naming conventions described in Chapter 1.

   Answer: ______________________________

2. Which field would make the most suitable primary key?

   Answer: ______________________________

3. Draw the button that you would click to make the current row into the primary key.

   Answer: [ ]

4 What is an **integer**?

Answer: ____________________

5 One field in the table shown has an unsuitable data type. Which?

Answer: ____________________

6 What field type should it have?

Answer: ____________________

7 Ring the row selector for **EventNumber** and label it with a **7**.

8 Describe how you would delete a field from the table structure.

Answer: ____________________

____

9 Describe how you would move the field **EventNumber** to the top of the field list.

Answer: ____________________

____

10 Ring the icon that you could use to insert a new row at the top of the table structure and label it with a **10**.

Sheet 2b Creating a New Database

(Extension work)

Name: ______________________________ **Date:** ______________

Look at the picture below and answer the questions.

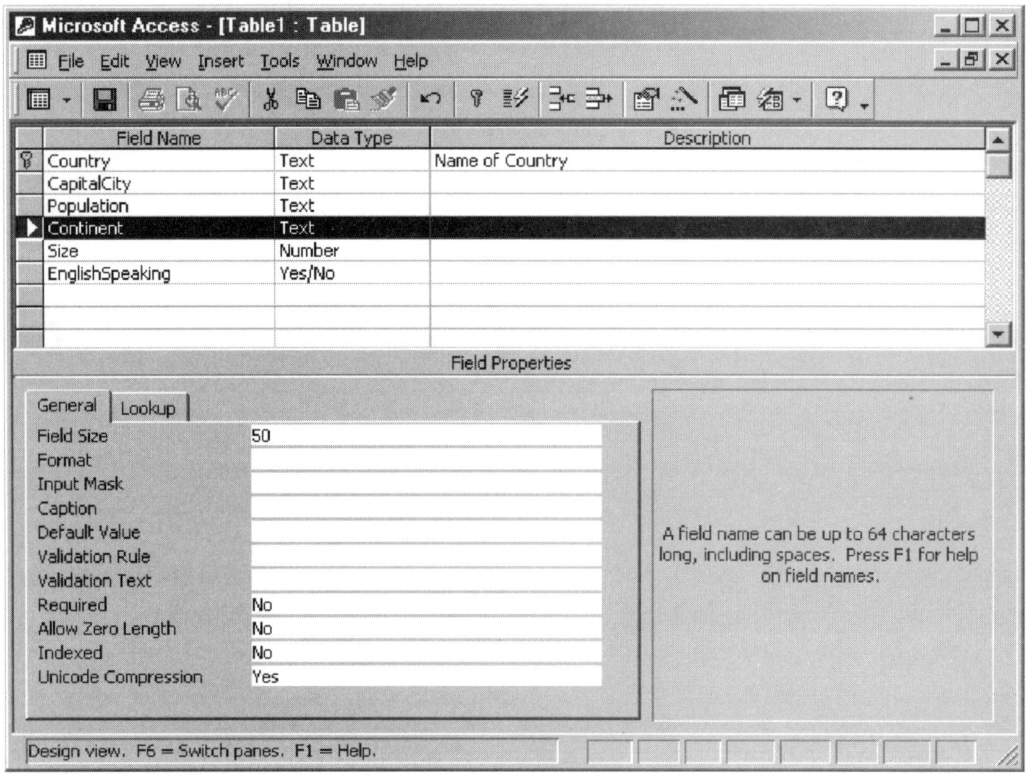

1. Which field is the primary key field?

   Answer: ______________________________

2. How would you remove the primary key symbol from a field?

   Answer: ______________________________

3. The **Population** field is going to hold the number of people living in the country. What data type should it be?

   Answer: ______________________________

4 How can you move **Continent** so that it appears as the second row of the table structure

Answer: ______________________________

5 How many different values can a field with a **Yes/No** data type hold?

Answer: ______________________________

6 Which **View** of the table is displayed above? Tick the correct answer below.

(a) Datasheet view ☐

(b) Design View ☐

(c) Table View ☐

7 How would you add a new field called **Coastline** under the field **CapitalCity?**

Answer: ______________________________

8 Circle the button you would click to save the table structure and label it with an **8**.

9 Suggest a suitable name for the table.

Answer: ______________________________

10 Circle the icon you could click to close the window and return to the Database window. Label it **10**.

Chapter 3

Datasheet View

Learning Objectives

- To open an existing database.
- To change between Datasheet and Design View.
- To enter data in a database table.
- To find, edit and delete data in a table.
- To add a new record.

New terms and vocabulary

Datasheet View, record selectors, wildcards.

Preparation

Photocopy Sheet 3a, Sheet 3b (Extension work) for each pupil. The worksheets can be completed away from the computer.

The pupils need to load the database that they created in the previous chapter. There is a fair amount of data entry in this chapter and the database will be used in all subsequent chapters so it needs to be saved carefully.

What to do

In this chapter pupils are introduced to different Table views that can be used when making changes to the database. In Chapter 1 we stressed the importance of distinguishing between the database structure and the data that was to be held in the database. The pupils have to remember that Design view is used to edit the database structure and Datasheet view is used to edit the data held in the database.

The pupils get some practice entering data into the database – you need to allow plenty of time for this as data entry speeds can vary considerably. The pupils can then find, edit, add and delete data in the table as described in the Pupil's book. Some of the techniques described would not be needed for a very small database, but pupils should understand that commercially-used databases can run into hundreds of thousands of records.

Pupils can enter an extra line of data at the end of the database with their own name, so that when a table is printed they will be able to distinguish their own work.

The Autonumber field is allocated automatically by Access and cannot be changed, so if a record is deleted and another one added, records may end up with a different number from the one shown in the screenshots. This does not matter.

Give out the first worksheet (Sheet 3a). Sheet 3b (Extension work) can be used as an extra activity.

Sheet 3a Datasheet View

(Classwork)

Name: ______________________________ **Date:** ______________

Look at the screenshot below and answer the questions.

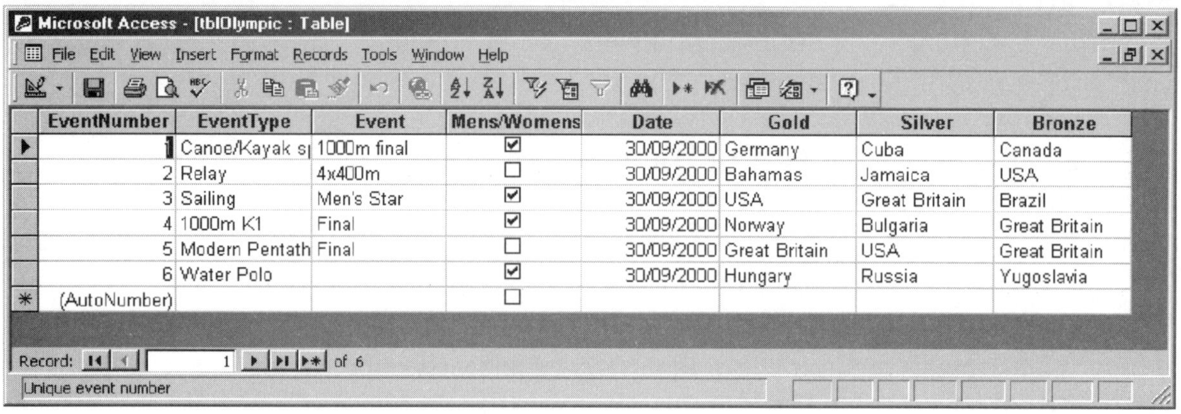

1 Which view of the database is shown in the screenshot above?

Answer: ______________________________

2 Can you change the number in the **EventNumber** field?

Answer: ______________________________

3 The field **Mens/Womens** has been given a data type of **Yes/No.** Describe two ways of putting a tick in the field to set it to **Yes.**

Answer: (i) ______________________

(ii) ______________________

4 What shortcut key combination can you use to put the same text or value as the field in the previous record?

Answer: ______________________________

5 Circle the **New Record** icon and label it with a **5**.

---

6 How can you widen the column for **EventType**?

Answer:____

____

---

7 Circle and label with a **7**, the **record selectors**.

---

8 Suppose the database had several hundred records. Circle the icon that you could use to help you find the first record in which a competitor from Great Britain is the Gold Medal winner. Label it with an **8**.

---

9 Describe how you would delete Record number 3.

Answer:____

____

---

10 Circle and label with a **10**, the record selector that you would use to go to the first record.

Sheet 3b Datasheet View

(Extension work)

Name: ______________________________ **Date:** ______________

Look at the screenshot below and answer the questions.

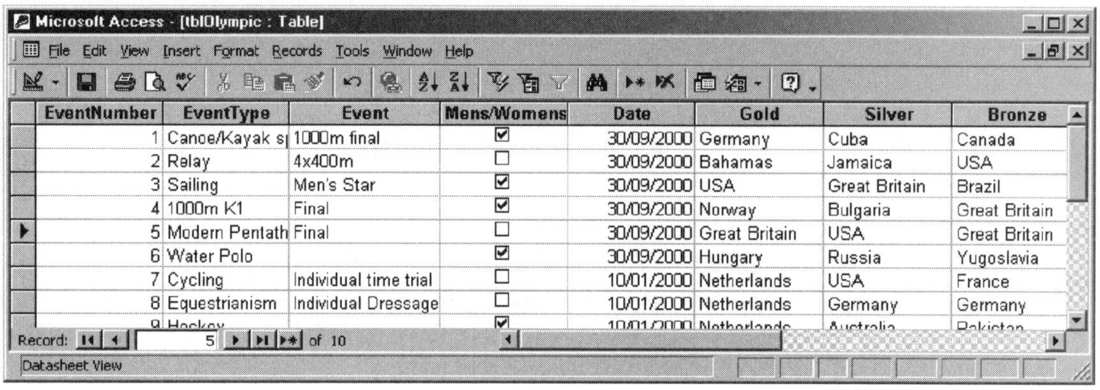

Screenshot 1

1 How many records are there in the database? Circle and label with a **1** the part of the screen that gives you the answer.

Answer: ____

____

2 Which record is currently selected?

Answer: ____

____

3 Circle and label with a **3** the icon you would click to return to Design view.

____

4 Circle and label with a **4** the icon you could press to delete the current record.

____

5 Circle and label with a **5** the icon you could press to go to the last record in the table.

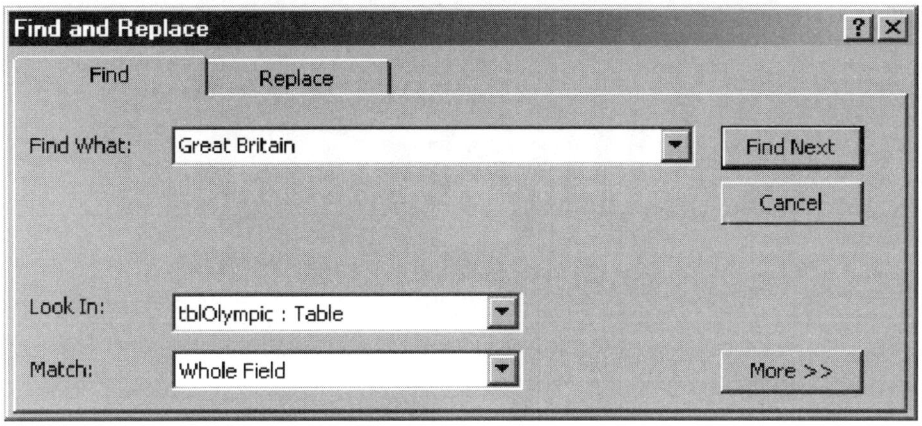

Screenshot 2

6 In Screenshot 1, circle and label with a **6** the first field that will be found when **Find Next** is pressed in Screenshot 2.

---

7 What will happen if you press **Find Next** a second time?

Answer: ______________________________

____

---

8 What could you enter in the **Find What** box to find the next record beginning with the letters **Ge**?

Answer: ______________________________

---

9 Describe how to find the first record showing **Great Britain** in the **Gold** column.

Answer: ______________________________

____

Chapter **4**

Data Validation

Learning Objectives

- To learn the meaning and importance of data validation.
- To learn the various types of validation rule that can be applied to fields in an Access database.
- To enter validation rules and validation text.
- To test the validation rules by entering invalid data.

New terms and vocabulary

Validation, validation rules.

Preparation

Photocopy Sheet 4a, Sheet 4b (Extension work) for each pupil. The worksheets can be completed away from the computer.

Read through the chapter and familiarise yourself with the data validation rules that Access allows, and the method of entering them. You will find, for example, that when you enter a validation rule for a date such as

Between 01/01/84 and 31/12/1991

Access encloses the dates between # signs. (See Figure 4.1 in the Pupil's book.) You do not have to enter these symbols yourself although you may do so.

If when entering data, you have entered an invalid field and want to abandon the record before reaching the end of the line, press **Esc** twice.

The pupils will need the database they have been working on in previous lessons.

What to do

This is quite a short chapter but it is an important one. Data validation is an important topic and one which crops up regularly on the National Curriculum and schemes of work (for example, *Year 7, Unit 5: Designing structure, capturing and presenting data*). You should explain that data validation involves defining rules so that the computer can check that the data entered is reasonable. It cannot always check that it is completely accurate. For example, the age of each pupil in a year 7 class may be given a validation rule

Age > 11 and Age < 14

The computer cannot ensure that the correct age is entered for James or Rebecca, only that a reasonable age has been entered. Likewise, you can attach a validation rule

Sex = 'M' or 'F'

but it is still possible to enter James's sex as F.

Try to think up several validation rules which can be given to different sets of data. The symbols used (<, >, etc) are given in the Pupil's book.

Give out the first worksheet (Sheet 4a). Sheet 4b (Extension work) can be used as an extra activity.

Sheet 4a Data Validation

(Classwork)

Name: ______________________ **Date:** ______________

The screenshot below shows a database of James Bond videos.

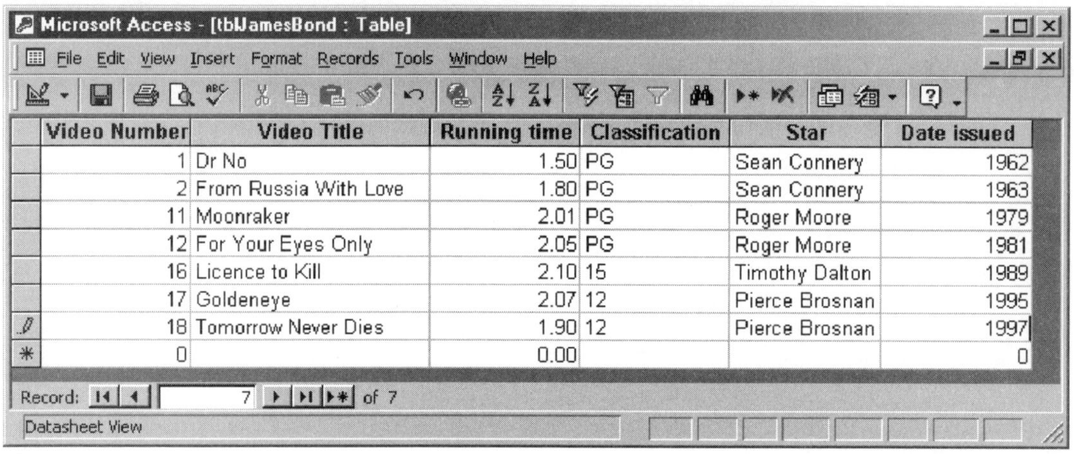

Video Number	Video Title	Running time	Classification	Star	Date issued
1	Dr No	1.50	PG	Sean Connery	1962
2	From Russia With Love	1.80	PG	Sean Connery	1963
11	Moonraker	2.01	PG	Roger Moore	1979
12	For Your Eyes Only	2.05	PG	Roger Moore	1981
16	Licence to Kill	2.10	15	Timothy Dalton	1989
17	Goldeneye	2.07	12	Pierce Brosnan	1995
18	Tomorrow Never Dies	1.90	12	Pierce Brosnan	1997
0		0.00			0

1. There are 7 videos in the database at the moment. As new videos are issued, they will be added to the database, each one being given a unique number between 1 and 30.
Write a suitable validation rule for **Video Number**.

   Answer: ______________________________

2. Would it be a good idea to add a validation rule to **Video Title**? Explain your answer.

   Answer: ______________________________

   ____

3. The Running time for the videos is always between $1\frac{1}{2}$ and $2\frac{1}{2}$ hours. Write a suitable validation rule for **Running Time**.

   Answer: ______________________________

4. The **Classification** is always one of **U, 12, 15** or **PG**. Write a validation rule.

   Answer: ______________________________

   ____

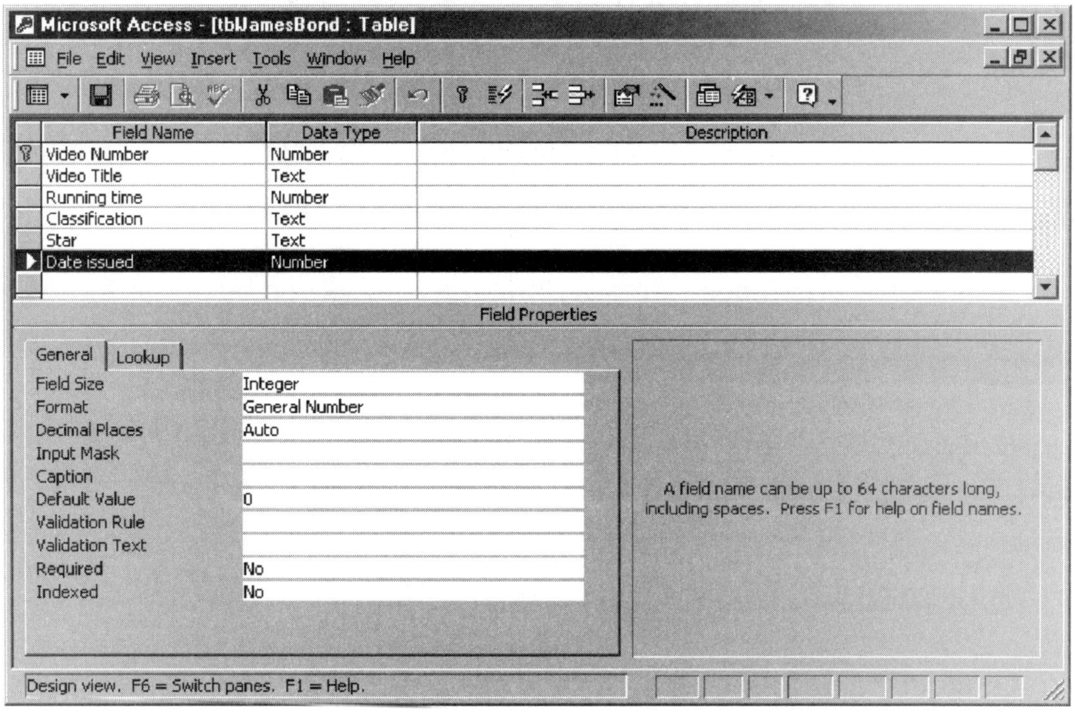

5 On the screenshot above, ring and label with a **5** where you would enter a validation rule for **Date Issued.**

---

6 What would be a suitable validation rule for **Date Issued**?

Answer: ____

---

7 What would be suitable validation text for Date Issued?

Answer: ____

____

---

8 On the screenshot above, ring and label with an **8** where you would enter validation text for **Date Issued.**

---

9 When would the person entering data see the validation text for **Date Issued**?

Answer: ____

____

Sheet 4b Data Validation

(Extension work)

Name: ______________________________ **Date:** ______________

The database table below holds details of all the cars owned by a Hire Car company.

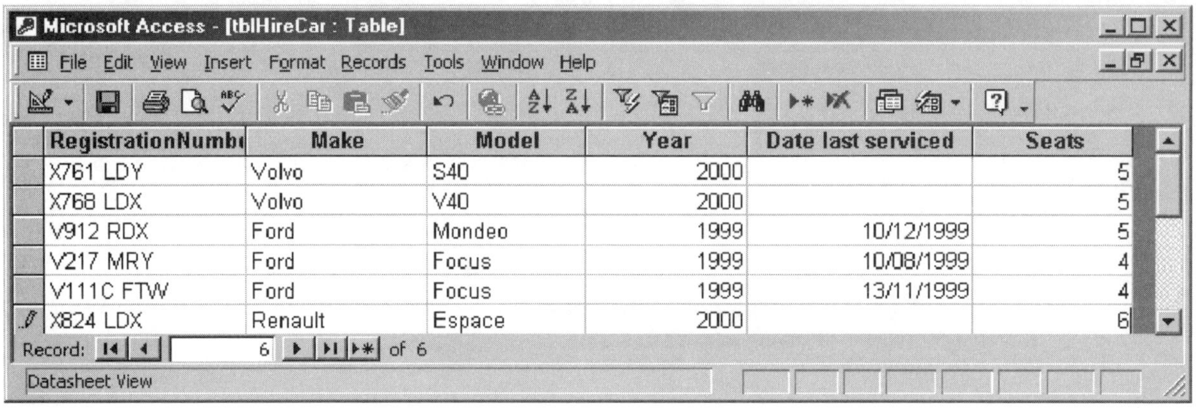

RegistrationNumb	Make	Model	Year	Date last serviced	Seats
X761 LDY	Volvo	S40	2000		5
X768 LDX	Volvo	V40	2000		5
V912 RDX	Ford	Mondeo	1999	10/12/1999	5
V217 MRY	Ford	Focus	1999	10/08/1999	4
V111C FTW	Ford	Focus	1999	13/11/1999	4
X824 LDX	Renault	Espace	2000		6

1. Which field is the key field?

   Answer: ______________________________

2. If this is the year 2000, and none of the cars owned by the Hire Car company is more than 2 years old, what would be a suitable validation rule for **Year**?

   Answer: ______________________________

3. What would be suitable validation text for **Year**?

   Answer: ______________________________

4. The company only ever buys Fords, Renaults and Volvos. What would be a suitable validation rule for **Make**?

   Answer: ______________________________

   ____

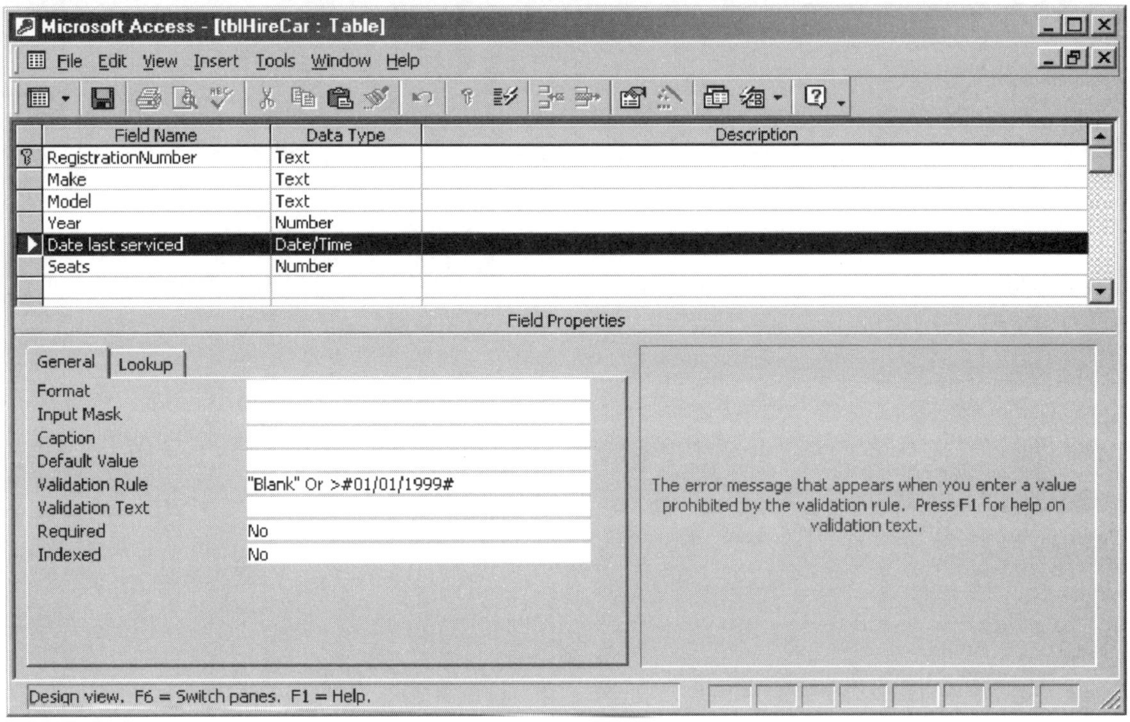

5 Which field does the validation rule shown in the screenshot above apply to?

Answer: ______________________________

6 Write some suitable validation text to accompany the validation rule shown.

Answer: ______________________________

____

7 Write a suitable validation rule for the field **Seats**, which shows the total number of seats including the driver's seat.

Answer: ______________________________

____

8 Draw a ring around the button that you would press to save the data structure and the new validation rules. Label it **8**.

Chapter **5**

Formatting and Printing

Learning Objectives

- To sort records on any field.
- To print a datasheet.
- To change the page layout from Portrait to Landscape.
- To hide and unhide columns in Datasheet View.
- To move columns.
- To adjust column widths.

New terms and vocabulary

Sort Ascending, Sort Descending, Print Preview, zoom, page selector.

Preparation

Photocopy Sheet 5a and 5b for each pupil. These worksheets can be completed away from the computer.

If the pupils are going to print their work you will need to make sure that a printer is available.

The pupils will need the Activities database that they have been working on in previous chapters.

What to do

Sorting an Access database is a very simple operation. You could compare this to sorting a manual database (e.g. a filing cabinet drawer) into alphabetical order which is a very time-consuming job. Let the pupils practise sorting on other fields such as date or currency fields, both ascending and descending.

It is a good idea for the pupils to get used to printing their datasheets in Landscape format as this means that the small, practice databases should fit on one page, saving paper and making them easier to read.

Beginners can easily forget about hidden fields (columns) and hidden rows (records) and become rather alarmed when they return to their datasheet after some time to find parts of it missing. Recommend to the pupils therefore that they unhide any information before closing their database.

If the pupils are going to print hard copy of their tables, make sure they have each added a record with their own name so that their work can be identified.

Give out the first worksheet (Sheet 5a). Sheet 5b (Extension work) can be used as an extra activity.

Sheet 5a Formatting and Printing

(Classwork)

Name: ______________________________ **Date:** ________________

The database table below holds details of all the cars owned by a Hire Car company.

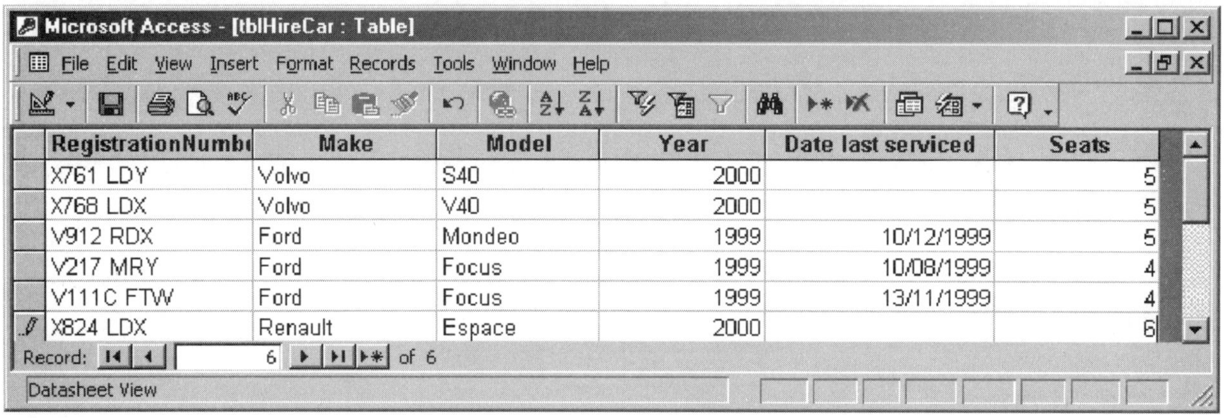

RegistrationNumb	Make	Model	Year	Date last serviced	Seats
X761 LDY	Volvo	S40	2000		5
X768 LDX	Volvo	V40	2000		5
V912 RDX	Ford	Mondeo	1999	10/12/1999	5
V217 MRY	Ford	Focus	1999	10/08/1999	4
V111C FTW	Ford	Focus	1999	13/11/1999	4
X824 LDX	Renault	Espace	2000		6

1. Suppose the pointer is somewhere in the second column. Circle and label with a **1**, the button you would press to sort the table in alphabetical order of Make.

2. Which field does Access automatically sort records on unless you specify otherwise?

   Answer: ______________________________

3. Describe how to sort the table so that the newest cars appear at the top of the table and the oldest at the bottom.

   Answer: ______________________________

   ____

4. Which menu and submenu option will you select to hide a column?

   Answer: ______________________________

5. On the screenshot, ring and label with a **5** the **Print Preview** button.

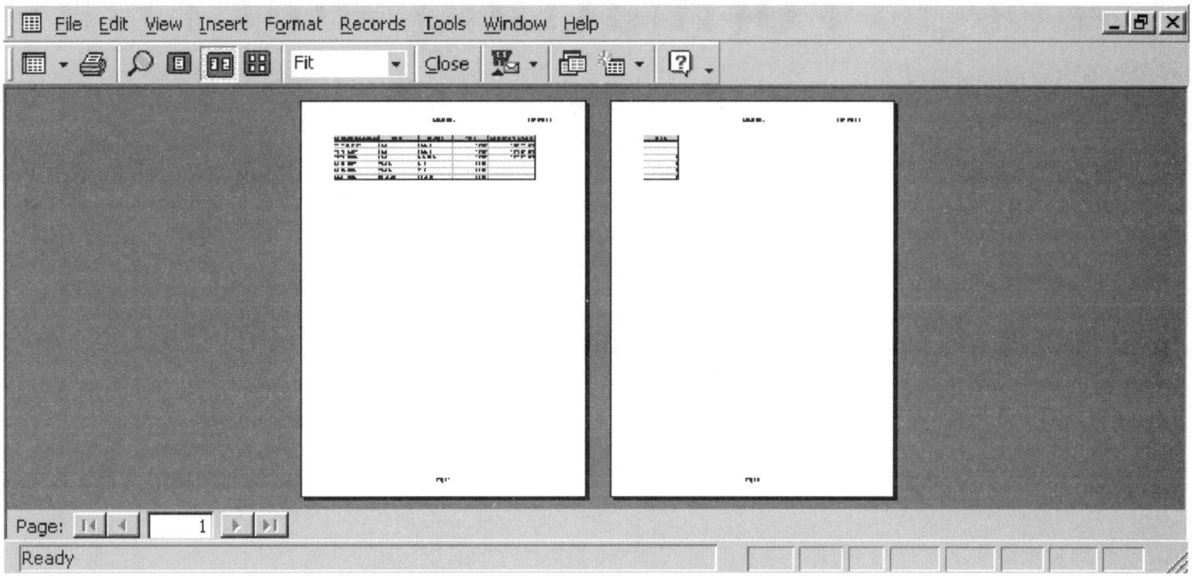

6 What view is shown in the screenshot above?

Answer: ____________________

7 Circle the button that you could press to return to Datasheet view. Label it with a **7**.

Answer: ____________________

8 Is the printout shown in Portrait or Landscape view?

Answer: ____________________

9 Circle the **Page selector** and label it with a **9**.

10 Circle the **Zoom** button and label it with a **10**.

Photocopiable free only to purchasing schools

Sheet 5b Formatting and Printing

(Extension work)

Name: ______________________________ **Date:** ______________

Look at the screenshot below and answer the questions.

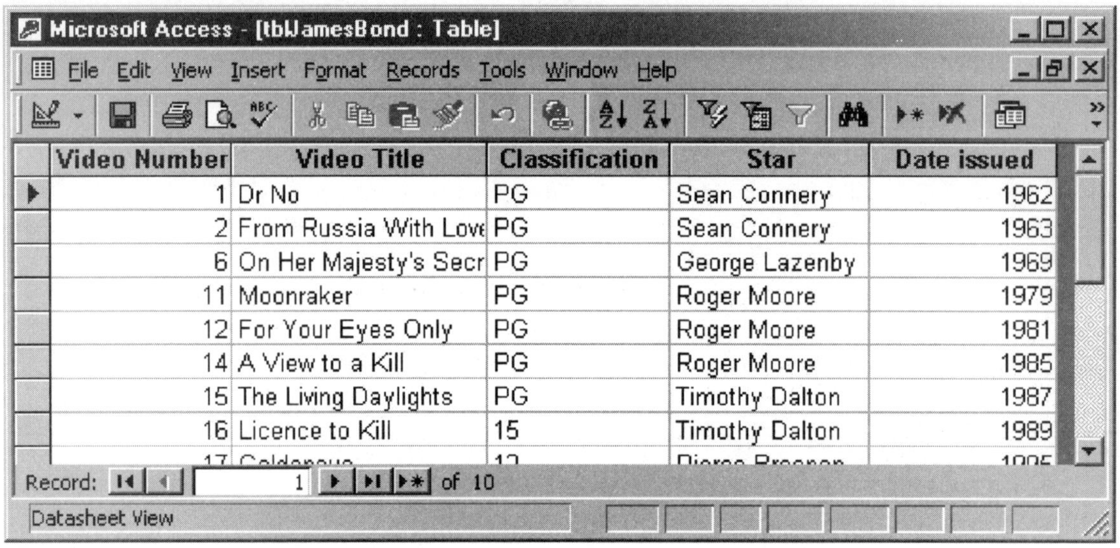

1 Suppose the pointer is somewhere in the last column. Circle and label with a **1** the button you would press to sort the table so that the most recent film appears at the top of the list.

---

2 How many records are there in the database?

Answer: ______________________________

---

3 Circle and label with a **3** where you could double-click to automatically adjust the **Video Title** column so that the whole title can be seen in every row.

Answer: ______________________________

---

4 One column has been hidden. How do you unhide it?

Answer: ______________________________

---

5 Circle and label with a **5** the button you could press to go to the last record in the database.

6 Why is it sensible to do a Print Preview before printing a hard copy of your table?

Answer: ____

____

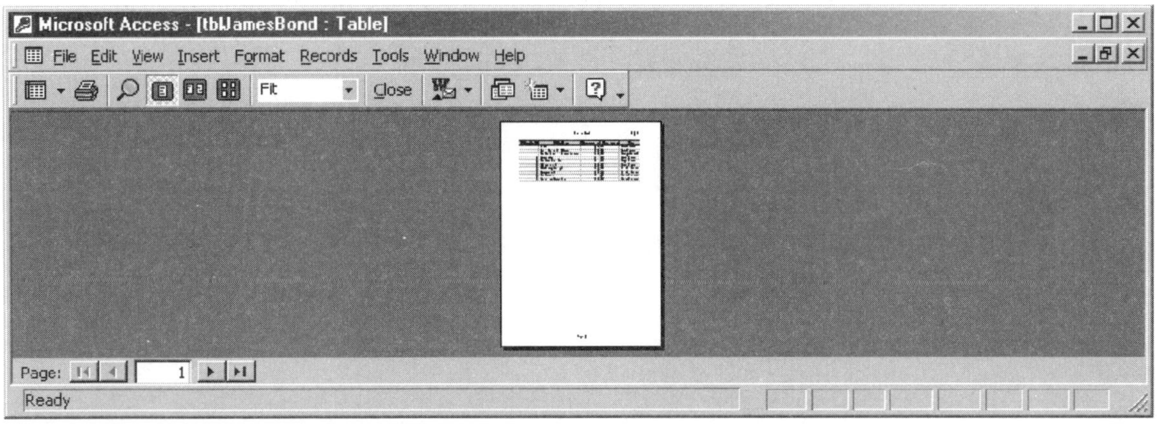

The screenshot above shows a Print Preview of the database.

7 Circle and label with a **7**, the button you would press to display 2 pages in the Preview.

8 What menu and submenu options would you select to change the page layout from Portrait to Landscape? Tick the correct answer.

(i) Format, Datasheet	☐	(iii) File, Page Setup	☐
(ii) Tools, Customize	☐	(iv) View, Pages	☐

9 Circle and label with a **9**, the button you would press to magnify the screen picture of the printed page so that you can read it.

10 Having magnified the page, how do you restore it to the previous size again?

Answer: ____

Chapter 6

Making Queries

Learning Objectives

- To understand the purpose of creating and saving queries.
- To select fields to appear in the query grid.
- To set simple criteria.
- To set multiple criteria.
- To use comparison operators.
- To sort query results.
- To hide fields in the query results table.
- To print the results of a query.

New terms and vocabulary

Query, query grid, simple criteria, multiple criteria, results table (also called answer table), comparison operator.

Preparation

Photocopy Sheet 6a and Sheet 6b (Extension work) for each pupil. These worksheets can be completed away from the computer.

Go over the chapter to familiarize yourself with all the comparison operators used by Access, and the different ways of expressing query criteria. For example, to find all pupils who have signed up for abseiling or windsurfing, you can either enter the criteria on two separate lines as shown in Figure 6.6, or on one line as **"Windsurf"** or **"Abseil"**. Great care needs to be taken when entering multiple criteria.

The students will need the Activities database they have been working on in previous chapters.

What to do

Discuss with the pupils the use of queries for searching a database for particular information, e.g. analysing questionnaires, obtaining subsets of data and so on. Saving a query allows it to be run over and over again whenever required, perhaps after adding more data. Recommend that the standard naming convention is adhered to i.e. save the query with the prefix **qry**. It is useful to be able to quickly distinguish between a table and a query as a source of data when creating forms or reports.

You may need to remind the pupils again about the difference between Datasheet view and Design view. They must be in Design view to create the query, but the results will be displayed in Datasheet view.

Go over the comparison operators again with the class (summarised in Figure 4.1). You may like to point out some of the pitfalls of writing multiple criteria in queries. For example in Figure 6.6, if the criteria **Between #1/1/1985# and #31/12/1991#** is not entered onto the second line, an extra record will appear in the answer table for Tony Hodson, who did sign up for abseiling, but whose date of birth lies outside the range.

Note too that the query grid is also used in this chapter for sorting records and hiding columns. The methods used are different from those described in Chapter 5 for sorting and hiding.

Give out the first worksheet (Sheet 6a). Sheet 6b (Extension work) can be used as an extra activity.

Sheet 6a Making Queries

(Classwork)

Name: ____________________________________ **Date:** ________________

A database has been used to record the responses from pupils and staff at a school that is considering building a new Sports facility. Respondents are asked to choose the facility they would most like to see built – a football pitch and pavilion, a swimming pool, a cricket pitch and pavilion or an indoor sports hall. Some of the responses are shown below.

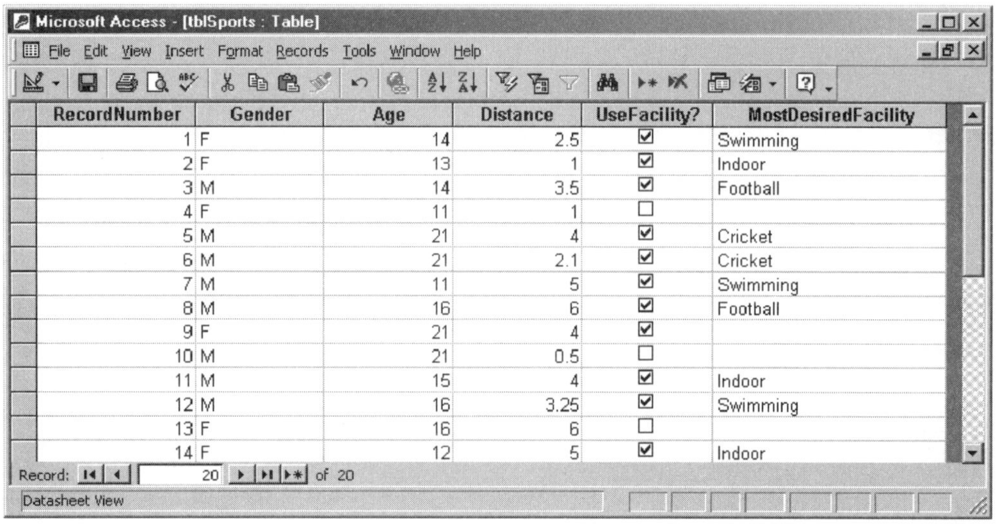

Microsoft Access - [tblSports : Table]

RecordNumber	Gender	Age	Distance	UseFacility?	MostDesiredFacility
1	F	14	2.5	☑	Swimming
2	F	13	1	☑	Indoor
3	M	14	3.5	☑	Football
4	F	11	1	☐	
5	M	21	4	☑	Cricket
6	M	21	2.1	☑	Cricket
7	M	11	5	☑	Swimming
8	M	16	6	☑	Football
9	F	21	4	☑	
10	M	21	0.5	☐	
11	M	15	4	☑	Indoor
12	M	16	3.25	☑	Swimming
13	F	16	6	☐	
14	F	12	5	☑	Indoor

Record: 20 of 20

Datasheet View

1 Which button could you double-click to return to the Database window? Circle it and label it **1**.

A new query is to be created. Some fields have been placed in the query grid as shown below.

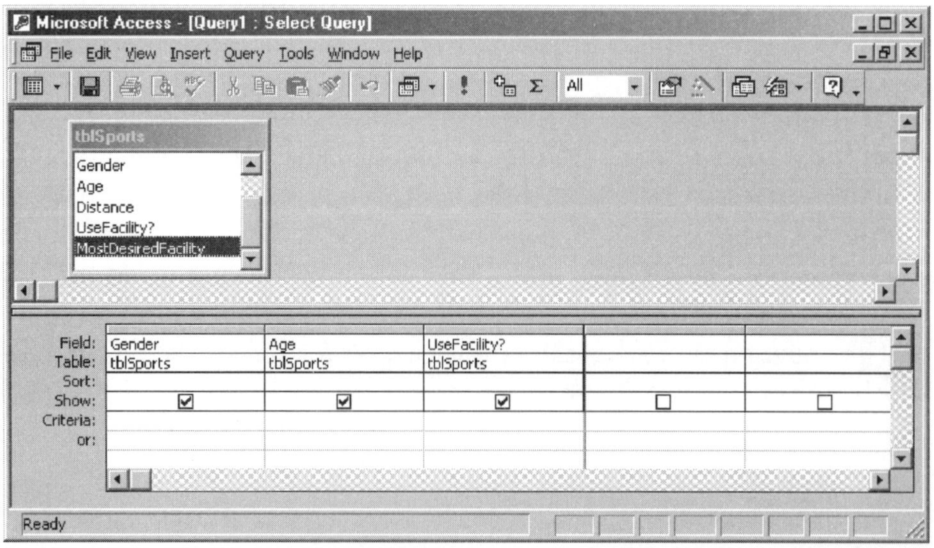

2 How would you place the field **MostDesiredFacility** in the Query grid?

Answer: ____

3 Fill in the query grid below to find all females in the survey.

Field:	Gender	Age	UseFacility?	MostDesiredFacility
Table:	tblSports	tblSports	tblSports	tblSports
Sort:				
Show:	☑	☑	☑	☑
Criteria:				
or:				

4 Fill in the query grid below to find all females whose preferred facility is **Swimming**.

Field:	Gender	Age	UseFacility?	MostDesiredFacility
Table:	tblSports	tblSports	tblSports	tblSports
Sort:				
Show:	☑	☑	☑	☑
Criteria:				
or:				

5 Fill in the query grid below to find all people who selected either **Football** or **Cricket** as their preferred activity.

Field:	Gender	Age	UseFacility?	MostDesiredFacility
Table:	tblSports	tblSports	tblSports	tblSports
Sort:				
Show:	☑	☑	☑	☑
Criteria:				
or:				

6 Fill in the query grid below to find all girls aged under 15 who selected **Indoor** as their preferred activity.

Field:	Gender	Age	UseFacility?	MostDesiredFacility
Table:	tblSports	tblSports	tblSports	tblSports
Sort:				
Show:	☑	☑	☑	☑
Criteria:				
or:				

7 How would you prevent the field **Gender** from being shown when you run the query?

Answer: ______________________________

8 On the second screenshot of the worksheet, circle and label with an **8** the button you would press to run your query.

Sheet 6b **Making Queries**

(Extension work)

Name: ______________________________ **Date:** ______________

Look at the screenshot below and answer the questions.

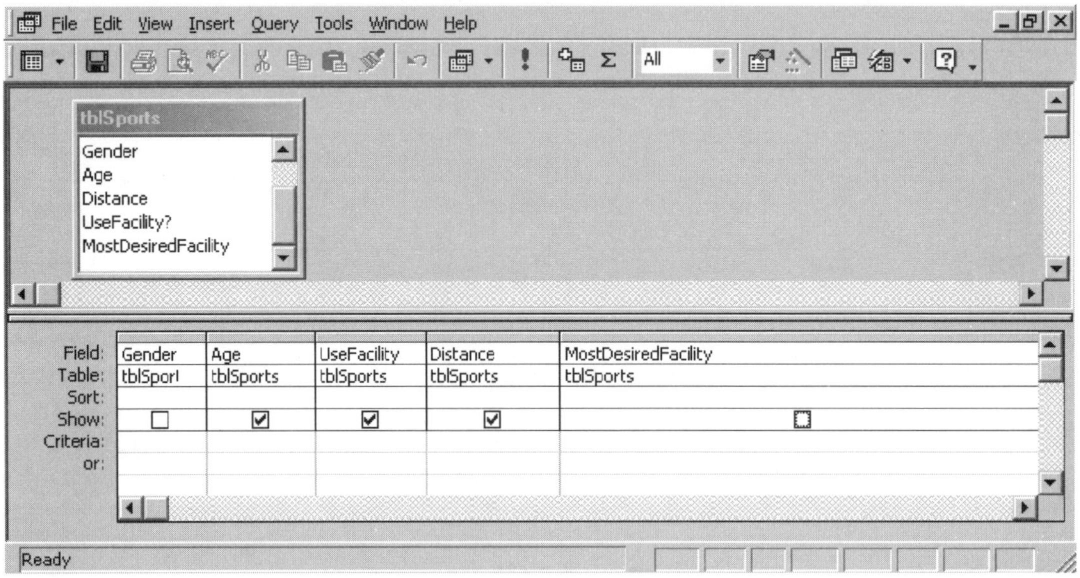

1 Suppose there are 100 records in the table tblSports. How many records will appear in the Answer table when this query is run?

Answer: ______________________________

2 Which fields will appear in the Answer table?

Answer: ______________________________

3 If you press the Save button, will you be saving the query itself, or the Answer table?

Answer: ______________________________

4 Circle and label with a **4** where you would click to sort the records in the Answer table on **Distance**.

5 Fill in the query grid below to find all people who live less than 4 miles from the planned Sports facility (given by the **Distance** field).

Field:	Gender	Age	UseFacility	Distance	MostDesiredFacility
Table:	tblSporl	tblSports	tblSports	tblSports	tblSports
Sort:					
Show:	☑	☑	☑	☑	☑
Criteria:					
or:					

---

6 Fill in the query grid below to find all people who live less than 4 miles from the planned Sports facility (given by the **Distance** field) and are aged 14 and over.

Field:	Gender	Age	UseFacility	Distance	MostDesiredFacility
Table:	tblSporl	tblSports	tblSports	tblSports	tblSports
Sort:					
Show:	☑	☑	☑	☑	☑
Criteria:					
or:					

---

7 The criteria below are designed to find all girls who selected either Swimming or Indoor facilities as their preferred choice. However the Answer table showed some boys in it. Amend the query so that it works as it should.

Field:	Gender	Age	UseFacility	Distance	MostDesiredFacility
Table:	tblSporl	tblSports	tblSports	tblSports	tblSports
Sort:					
Show:	☑	☑	☑	☑	☑
Criteria:	"F"				"Swimming"
or:					"Indoor"

---

8 **UseFacility** is a **Yes/No** field. Complete the query grid to find all boys who live between 5 and 10 miles from the planned facility and whose record has **Yes** in the **UseFacility** field.

Field:	Gender	Age	UseFacility	Distance	MostDesiredFacility
Table:	tblSporl	tblSports	tblSports	tblSports	tblSports
Sort:					
Show:	☑	☑	☑	☑	☑
Criteria:					
or:					

Chapter **7**

Presenting Data

Learning Objectives

- To understand what a report is and why reports are needed.
- To select fields to appear on a report.
- To edit a report format.
- To add a new field to a report.
- To print a report.
- To create a bar chart and pie chart.

New terms and vocabulary

Report, report format, report header, report footer, page header, page footer, Properties window, control source, bar chart, legend, pie chart.

Preparation

Photocopy Sheet 7a and Sheet 7b (Extension work) for each pupil. These worksheets can be completed away from the computer.

You should try out the chapter first and make sure that the graph feature is installed on your system. If not, you should be able to install an 'add-on' from the Microsoft Office software CD. The pupils will need the Activities database used in previous chapters.

What to do

Discuss with the pupils the differences between using a report and simply printing the data in Datasheet view as they did in Chapter 5. A report is far more flexible as it allows you to add your own headings, a date, page number, totals and so on. You can also format the text by choosing different fonts and font sizes.

The easiest way to create a report in Access is to use the wizard provided which asks you questions and creates a report based on your answers. Ensure that the pupils understand that reports can be based on tables or queries and that they should follow the standard naming convention and save reports with a name beginning **rpt.**

To edit the report pupils will have to revert to Design view. This can look rather confusing at first sight, so point out to the students the difference between the actual field and the field title (in bold). They can drag the fields to change their position or click on the field and use the alignment buttons on the toolbar to align the text within the field. Draw the pupils' attention to the format of the date and page number in the report footer.

More advanced pupils may want to change other properties of the form such as background colour, change the order of the fields or add a picture to the report. The pupils should be encouraged to experiment.

Discuss with the class the different types of chart that are available and which are most suitable for different situations. Continuous line graphs are best for continuously varying values such as a pupil's height measured at 3-monthly intervals from age 10 to 15, say. A bar chart is more suitable for showing, for example, total sales of each of 6 different items in a shop. (You don't want more than about 6 – 8 items on a bar chart or a pie chart.) A pie chart is useful for giving an instant picture of the fraction of a population in a survey who fit into each category – for example, the number of people who travel to school by bus, car, foot or cycle.

Give out the first worksheet (Sheet 7a). Sheet 7b (Extension work) can be used as an extra activity.

Sheet 7a Presenting Data

(Classwork)

Name: ______________________ **Date:** ____________

The screenshot below shows the format for a report to print the results of a questionnaire about planned Sports facilities.

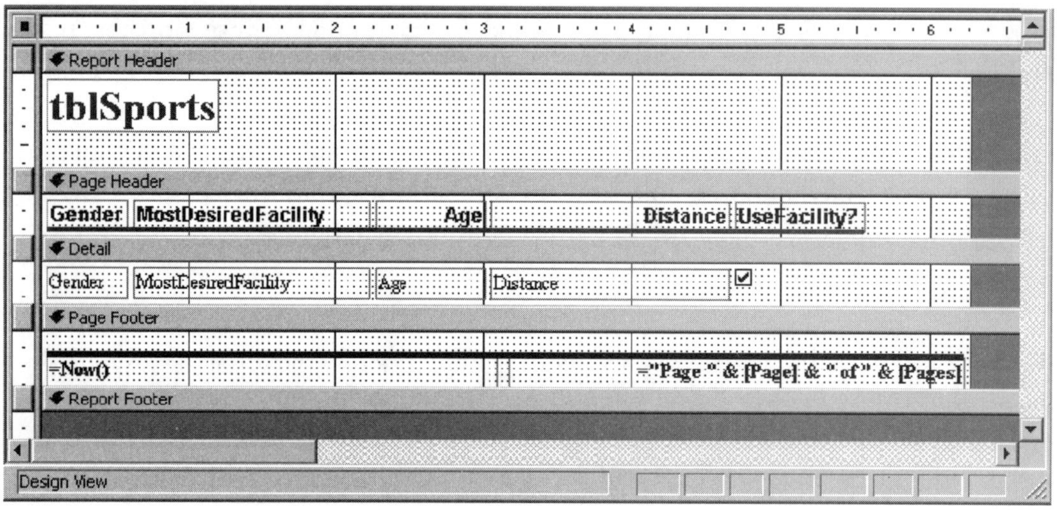

1. How would you change the report heading to **Results of Questionnaire.**

   Answer: ______________________

2. What will be displayed in the Page Footer section of the printed report?

   Answer: ______________ & ______________

3. What will be displayed in the **Detail** section of the report?

4. How would you make the heading and field **Distance** narrower?

   Answer: ______________________

5 The database user wants to present the data from the questionnaire in such a way that it is easy to see approximately what proportion of respondents favour a swimming pool. What would be the best way of showing this?

Answer:

(a) a printed report ☐ (b) a bar chart ☐

c) a pie chart ☐

The next few questions refer to the screenshot below. It depicts a chart showing the proportion of respondents who voted for each category of facility.

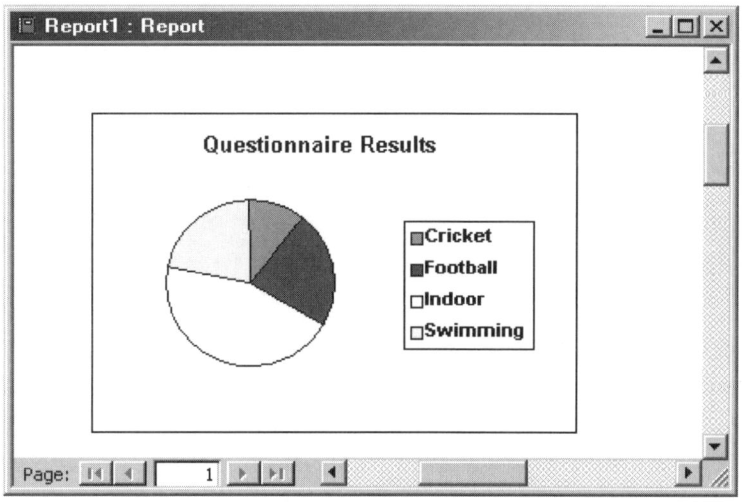

6 Approximately what percentage of the questionnaire respondents voted for **Football** sports facilities?

Answer: ______________________________

---

7 Circle the legend in the above picture and label it with a **7**.

Answer: ______________________________

---

8 Name another type of chart that could have been used to show the number of people voting for each facility.

Answer: ______________________________

____

Photocopiable free only to purchasing schools

Sheet 7b Presenting Data

(Extension work)

Name: ______________________ **Date:** ______________

The screenshot below shows the cars owned by a car hire company.

RegistrationNumber	Make	Model	Year	Date last serviced	Seats
V111 FTW	Ford	Focus	1999	13/11/1999	4
V217 MRY	Ford	Focus	1999	10/08/1999	4
V912 RDX	Ford	Mondeo	1999	10/12/1999	5
W441 DRU	Renault	Clio	1999	03/03/2000	4
W442 DRU	Renault	Clio	1999	15/03/2000	4
W579 DRY	Ford	Mondeo	1999	07/01/2000	5
W580 DRY	Ford	Mondeo	1999	17/02/2000	5
W581 DRY	Ford	Focus	1999	28/04/2000	4
X761 LDY	Volvo	S40	2000		5
X768 LDX	Volvo	V40	2000		5
X824 LDX	Renault	Espace	2000		6
*			0		0

1. The company wants to obtain a report of all cars that were last serviced before 1st April, 2000. Describe how to do this.

   Answer: ______________________________

A report is produced as shown below.

Microsoft Access

File Edit View Tools Window Help

Service Report

Service Report

Date last serviced	RegistrationNumber	Make	Model
10/08/1999	V217 MRY	Ford	Focus
13/11/1999	V111 FTW	Ford	Focus
10/12/1999	V912 RDX	Ford	Mondeo
07/01/2000	W579 DRY	Ford	Mondeo
17/02/2000	W580 DRY	Ford	Mondeo
03/03/2000	W441 DRU	Renault	Clio
15/03/2000	W442 DRU	Renault	Clio

Ready

2. What sequence is the report sorted in?

   Answer: ______________________________

3. Circle and label with a **3** the button you would press if you wanted to make changes to the report headings.

---

4. Circle and label with a **4** the button you would press to see the whole page on the screen.

---

5. What option do you choose in the Database window to create a chart? Tick the correct answer.

(i) Tables ☐ (iii) Reports ☐

(ii) Forms ☐ (iv) Pages ☐

The screenshot below shows a chart being created.

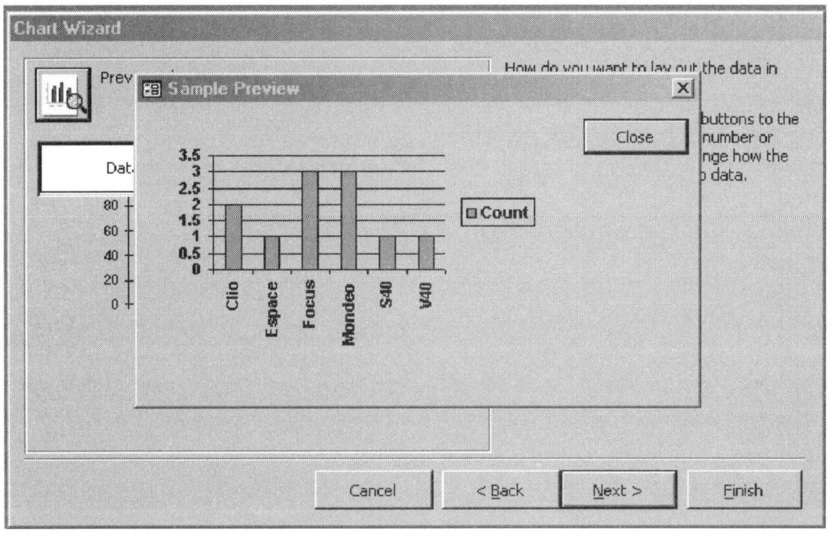

6. What type of chart is being created?

Answer: ______________________________

---

7. Is the legend needed for this chart?

Answer: ______________________________

---

8. What does the chart show?

Answer: ______________________________

Photocopiable free only to purchasing schools

Chapter **8**

Forms for Data Entry

Learning Objectives

- To create a form for data input.
- To use a form for data entry.
- To use a Combo box to allow the user to select from a number of options.
- To set a default value for a field.
- To change the tab order of fields on the form.

New terms and vocabulary

User interface, form, tailor a form, data input, Combo box, default value, tab order.

Preparation

Photocopy Sheet 8a and Sheet 8b (extension work) for each pupil. These worksheets can be completed away from the computer. The pupils will need the Activities database used in previous chapters.

What to do

Explain to the pupils the use of forms as a user interface for data entry as well as providing an additional method of data validation. The easiest way of creating a form is to use the Form Wizard provided with Access. In a similar way to the Report Wizard, it asks the user questions and produces the form based on the answers. Recommend the standard naming convention again – save the form with a name beginning with **frm.**

Explain to the pupils the difference between list boxes and combo boxes (a combination of list box and text box) and their use for speeding up data entry and eliminating typing errors. In the example in the pupil's book a combo box is used, which allows the user to select from a list or type in their own entry. In this particular case the table field also has a data validation applied to it so that only the values in the list can be entered and it therefore functions as a drop-down list. (A combo box property allowing list values only could also have been used if there was no field validation.)

This chapter covers just the basics of Form design – more advanced pupils may want to change the colour of the text or background, change the font, rearrange fields on the form and so on. Much of this is quite simple and the pupils should be encouraged to experiment. The **Properties** box shows the property of each object. You can display the properties of any object including the form itself by right-clicking on the object and selecting **Properties.**

Forms is the last topic in the book and when the pupils have completed this, they will have created a sample application that includes the basic elements of all databases – a table, data input form, queries and reports. They could be encouraged to write a User Guide for the project explaining to the user how to use the system.

The next stage is to apply the techniques learned to projects of their own!

Give out the first worksheet (Sheet 8a). Sheet 8b (extension work) can be used as an extra activity.

Sheet 8a Forms for Data Entry
(Classwork)

Name: ______________________ **Date:** __________

The screenshot below shows a data entry form for entering James Bond videos into a database.

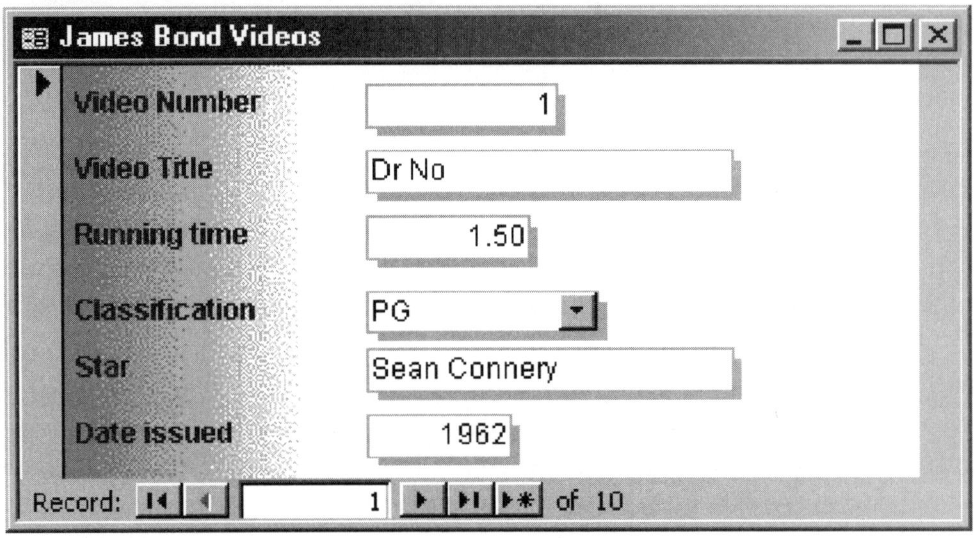

1 What type of box is used for entering **Classification**?

Answer: ______________________

2 Name two advantages of using this type of box for **Classification**.

Answer: ______________________

____

3 When the user types an entry using this form, the cursor jumps from **Running Time** to **Star**. What does the form designer need to change?

Answer: ______________________

4 Circle the button you would click to add a new record. Label it with a **4**.

Answer: ______________________

The screenshot below shows the same form in Design View.

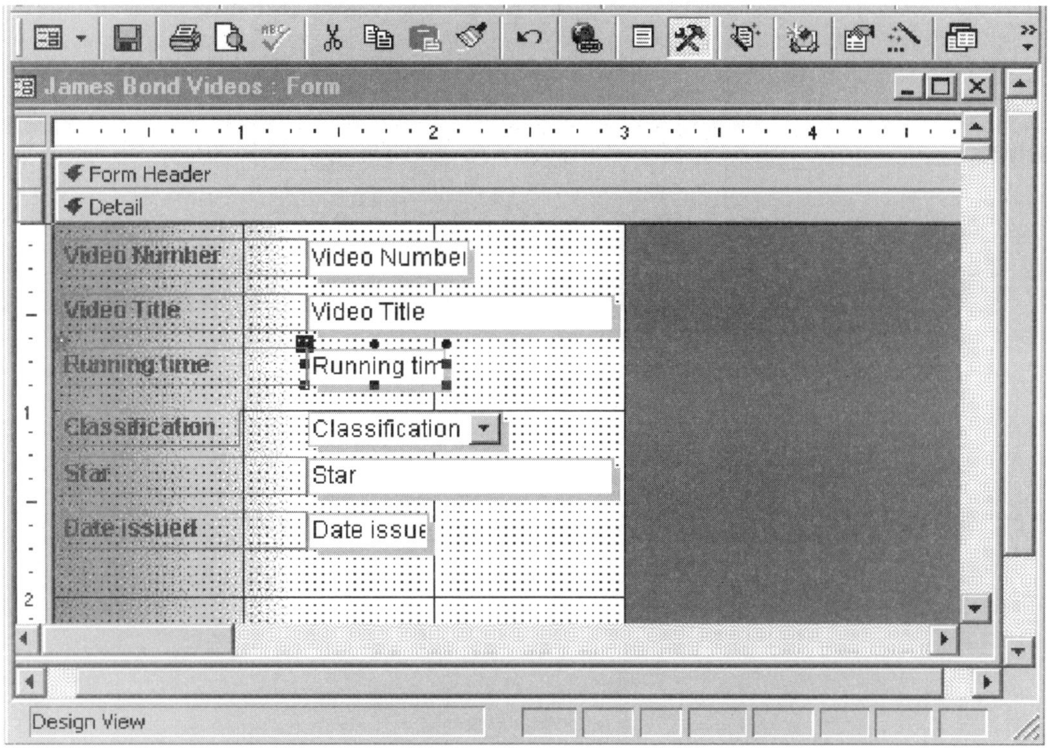

5 How would you move the label and field **Running Time** to the bottom of the form?

Answer: ____

---

6 How could you make the field **Running Time** narrower?

Answer: ____

---

7 Circle where you could drag to make the form wider and label it with a **7**.

---

8 Circle the **Properties** icon and label it with an **8**.

Sheet 8b Forms for Data Entry

(Extension work)

Name: ______________________ **Date:** ____________

Look at the screenshot below and answer the questions.

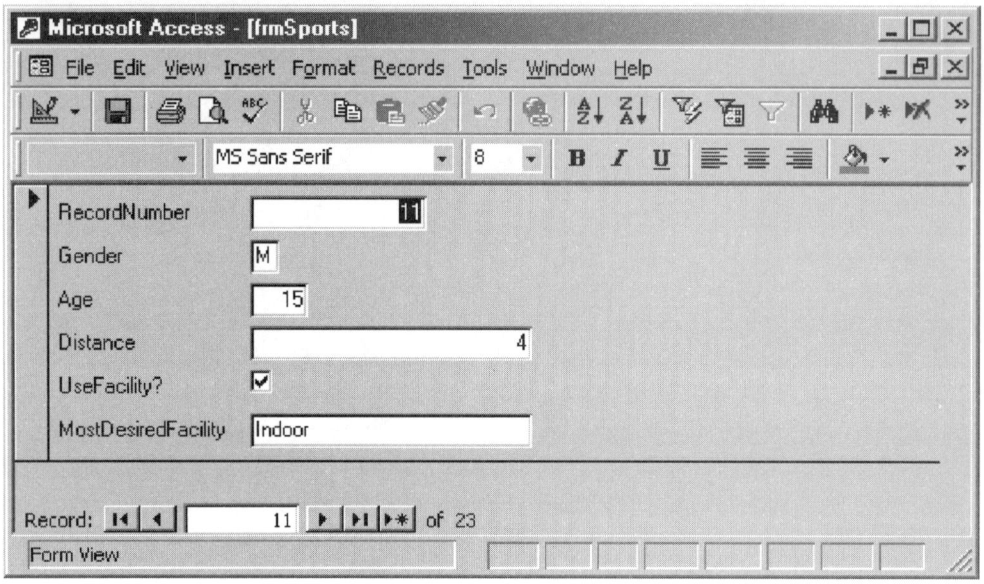

1. How can you move quickly to the first record in the database?

   Answer: ______________________

2. Circle the **Find** icon and label it with a **2**

3. Describe how you could use the **Find** button to find the next record with the **Gender** field set to **F**.

   Answer: ______________________

4. Ring and label with a **4**, the button you would click to make changes to the design of the form.

5. Describe how you could delete the current record.

   Answer: ______________________

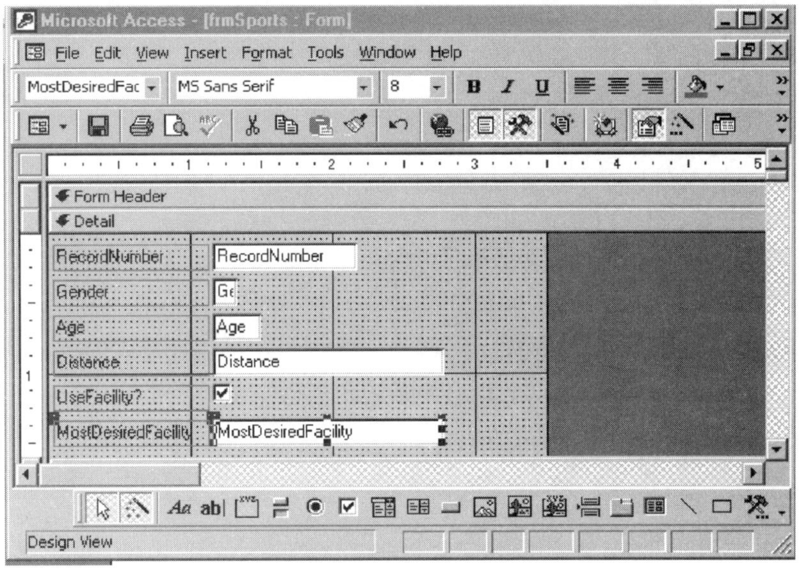

6 Describe how you would make the **Age** label narrower.

Answer: ______________________________

7 Name a field that could usefully be made into a Combo box.

Answer: ______________________________

8 Ring and label with an **8** the button you would click on the toolbar at the bottom of the screen to create a combo box.

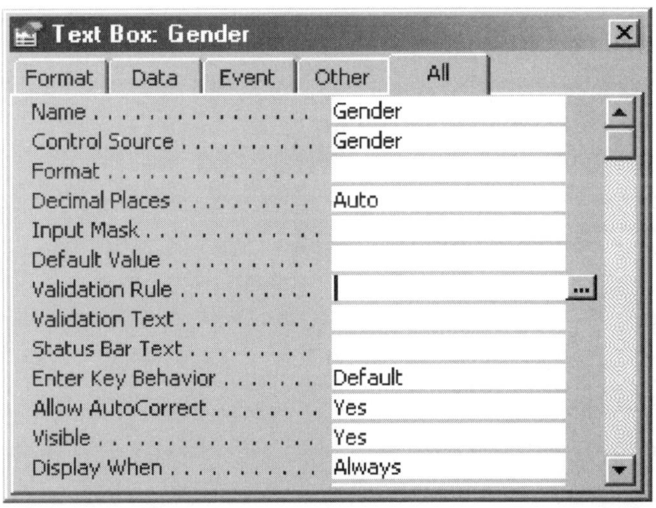

9 Circle and label with a **9** where you would enter a Default value in the Properties box shown above.

10 Enter a suitable validation rule for **Gender** in the Properties box above.

Answer: ______________________________

Answers

Sheet 1a Introduction to Databases

1. 5.
2. 6
3. Text.
4. Currency.
5. Date/Time.
6. AutoNumber (accept Number or Integer).
7. tblPetVisits or something similar.
8. Date of Birth, Sex, Notes, Description, Breed, Owner's name / address / telephone number, (Accept any other reasonable suggestion).
9. Date/Time for Date of Birth (note that Age is not a good idea for a field because it has to be updated every year).
   Text for most other fields.
10. Date of last visit.

Sheet 1b Introduction to Databases

1. 4.
2. 5.
3. Text.
4. Currency.
5. Number (integer).
6. Text.
7. tblStock or something similar.
8. Cost Price, Size, Reorder level, Supplier, (Any other reasonable suggestion).
9. Currency for Cost Price, Text or Number for Size, Number for Re-order level, Text for Supplier.
10. ProductCode, ProductDescription, QuantityInStock.

Sheet 2a Creating a New Database

1. tblOlympics, tblEvents or something similar.
2. EventNumber.
3. 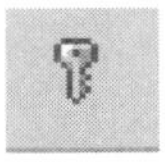
4. A whole number, without a decimal point.
5. **NumberOfCompetitors**
6. It should be Number.
7. See figure.
8. Click on the row selector and press the **Delete** key.
9. Click on the row selector and drag it to the new position.
10. See figure.

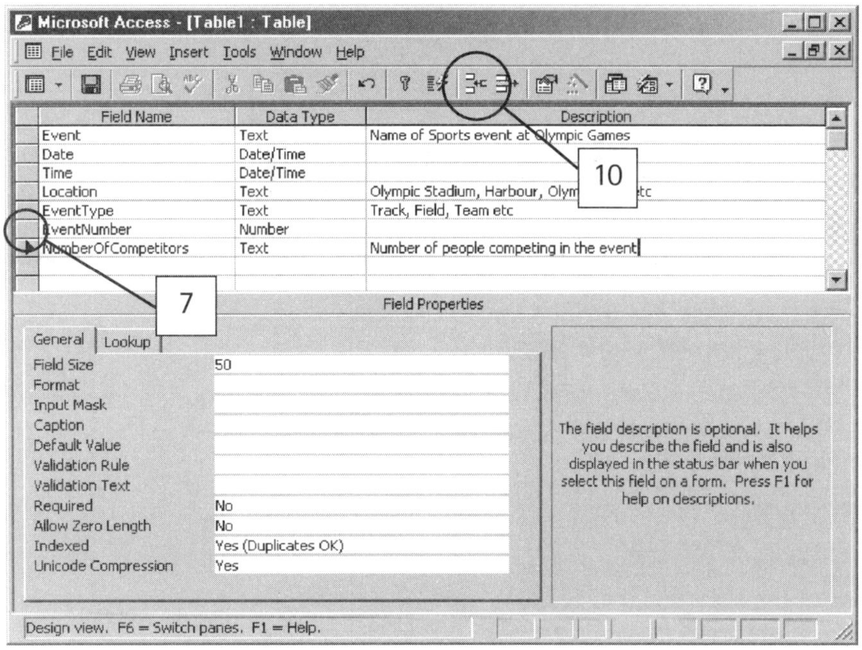

Sheet 2b Creating a New Database

1. Country.
2. Select the primary key row and click the **Primary Key** icon.
3. Number.
4. Click on the row selector and drag it to the new position.
5. Two.
6. b)
7. Click the **Population** row selector, then click the **Insert** icon. 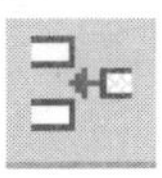
8. See figure.
9. tblCountry or something similar.
10. See figure.

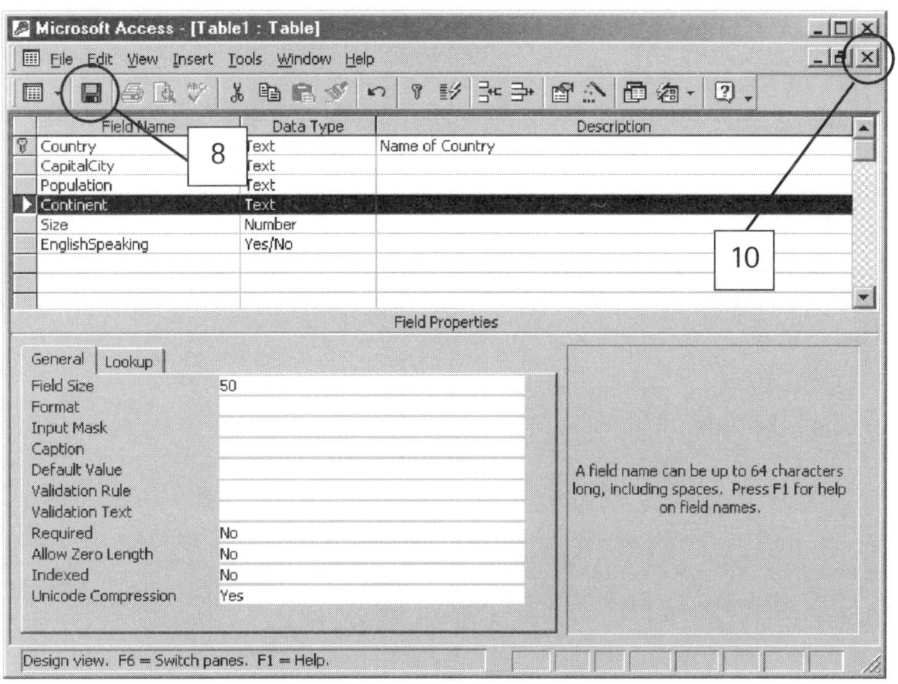

Sheet 3a Datasheet View

1. Datasheet View.
2. No.
3. Click in the box or press Spacebar. (A tick means it is a Men's event, a blank means it is a Women's event).
4. **Ctrl** + ' (apostrophe).
5. See figure. (**New Record** icon.) Also allow the one in the record selectors.
6. Drag the right side of the column header.
7. See figure.
8. See figure. (**Find** icon)
9. Select the record and click on the **Delete** icon.
10. See figure.

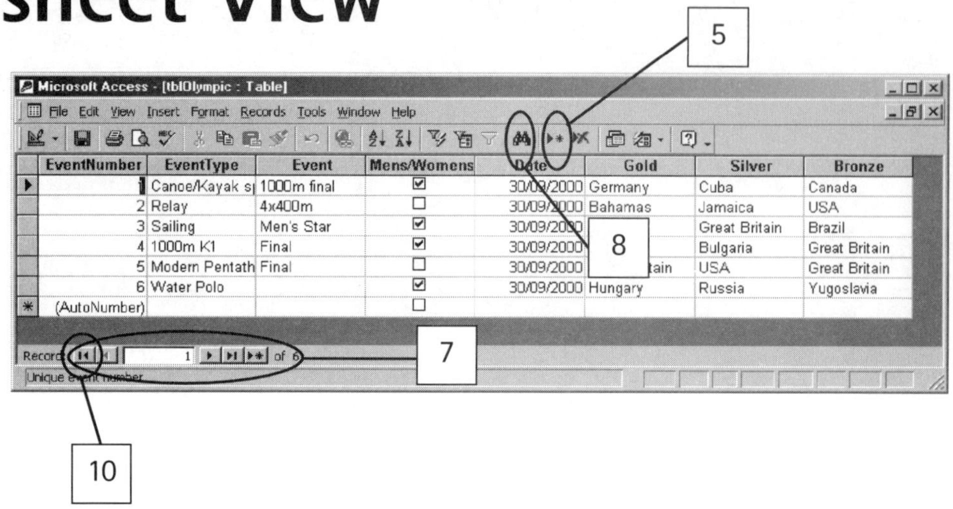

Sheet 3b Datasheet View

1. 10 - see figure.
2. 5.
3. See figure.
4. See figure.
5. See figure.
6. See figure.
7. It will find Great Britain in record 5, **Gold** field.
8. **Ge***.
9. Select the **Gold** column before doing the Find.

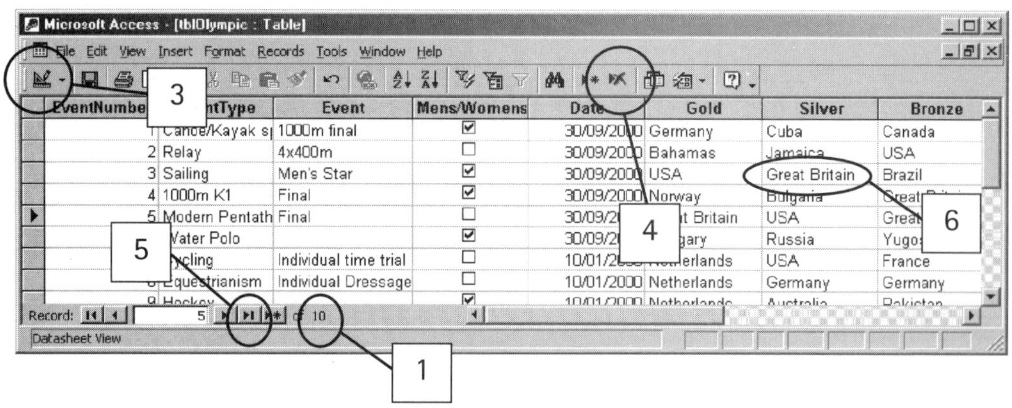

Sheet 4a Data Validation

1. **Between 1 And 30;**
   >0 And <31.
2. No. The validation rule would have to be a long string of all the possible titles.
3. **Between 1.5 And 2.5.**
4. **"U" Or "12" Or "15" Or "PG"**
5. See figure.
6. **>1961; >=1962**
7. "Date cannot be before 1962"
8. See figure.
9. On moving to another field or record after entering an invalid value for Date Issued.

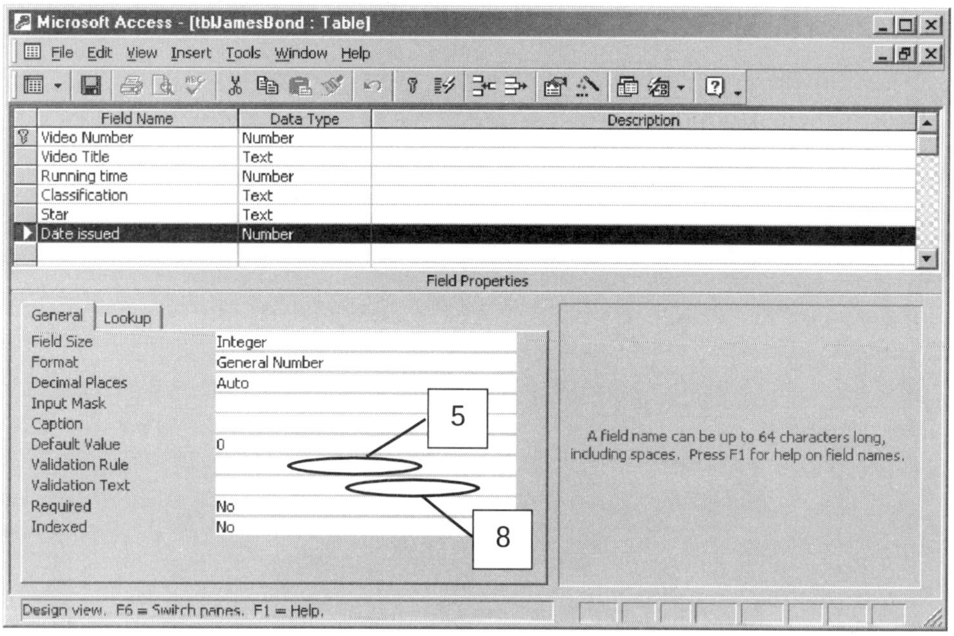

Sheet 4b Data Validation

1. **RegistrationNumber.**
2. **> 1997** or **>= 1998.**
3. The car must not be more than 2 years old.
4. **"Ford" Or "Renault" Or "Volvo"**
5. **Date last serviced.**
6. "Date cannot be before 1999"
7. **<= 5** or any reasonable answer.
8. See figure.

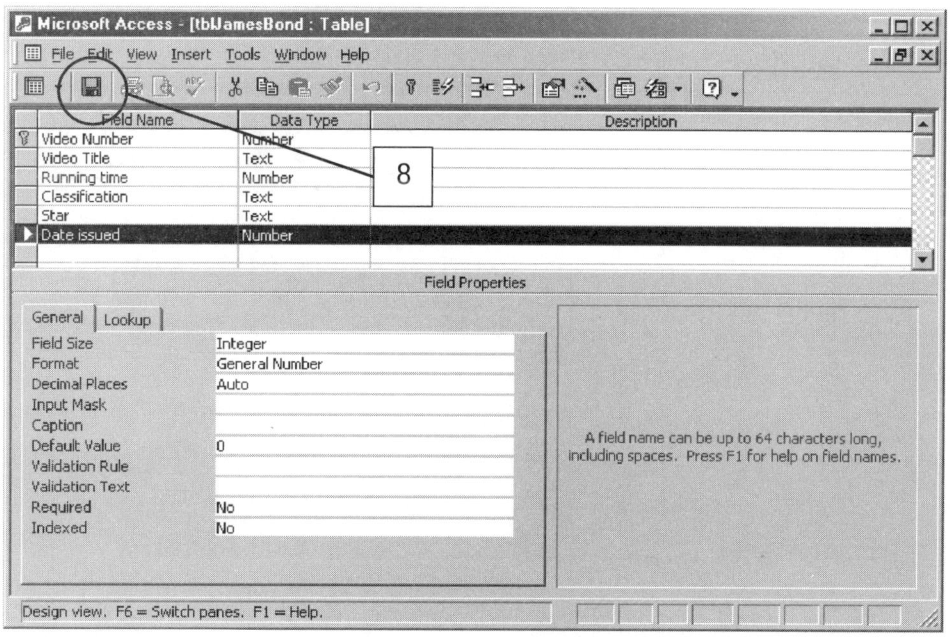

Sheet 5a Formatting and Printing

1. See figure.
2. The key field.
3. Click the Sort Descending button on the toolbar.
4. **Format, Hide Column.**
5. See figure.
6. Print Preview.
7. See figure.
8. Portrait.
9. See figure.
10. See figure.

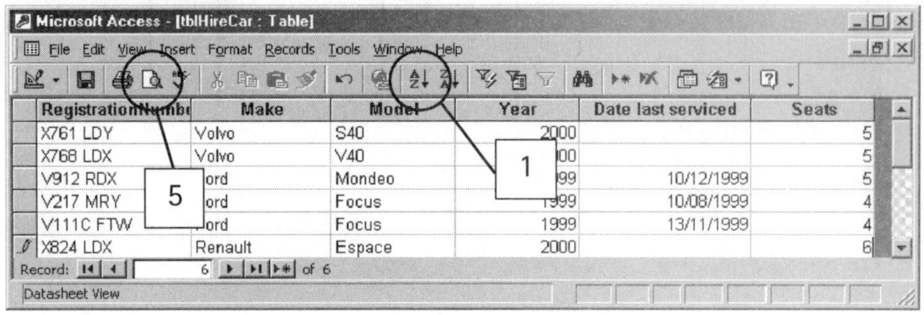

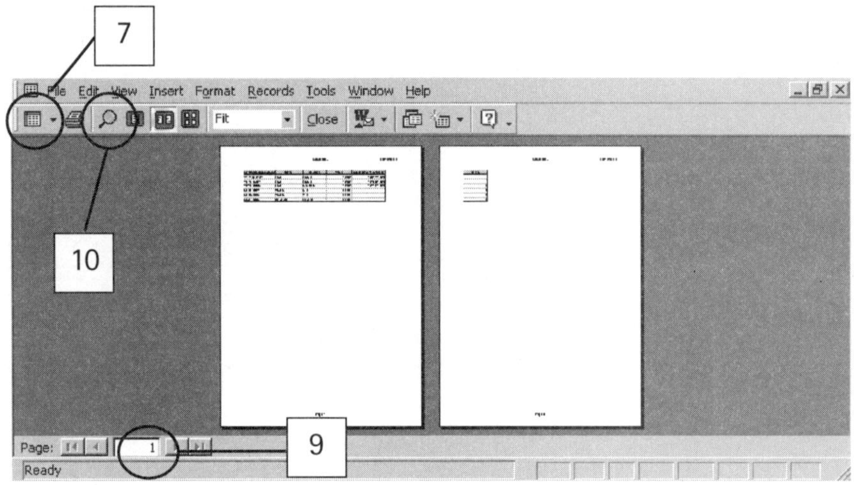

Sheet 5b Formatting and Printing

1. See figure.
2. 10 (some have obviously been deleted).
3. See figure.
4. **Format, Unhide Column.**
5. See figure.
6. To avoid wasting paper.
7. See figure.
8. iii.
9. See figure.
10. Click on it.

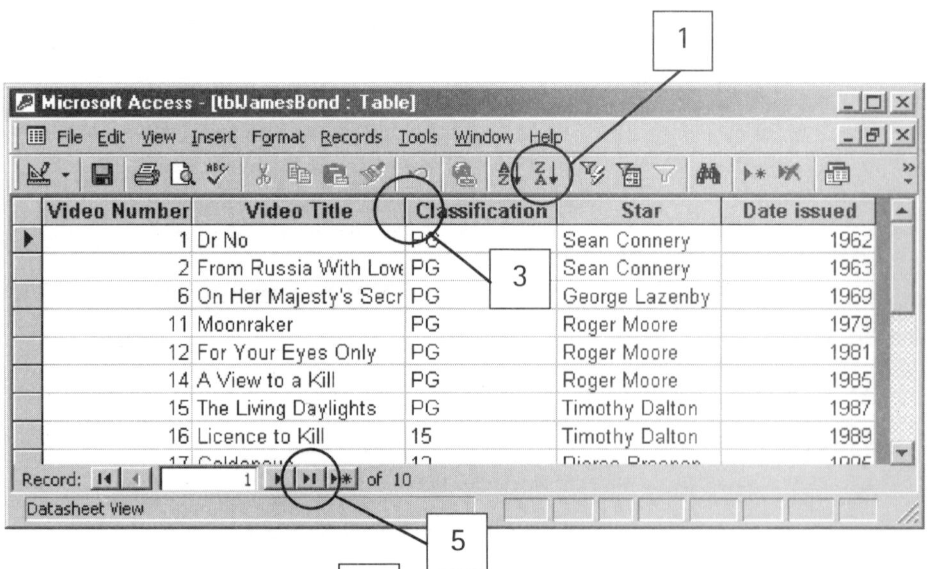

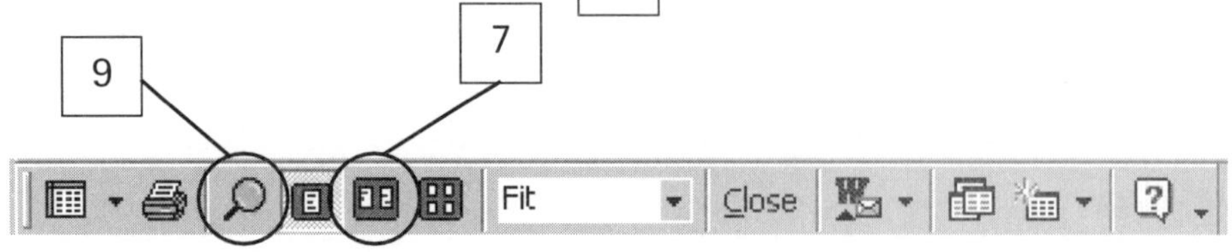

Sheet 6a Making Queries

1. See figure.
2. Double-click on it or drag it onto the grid.
3. Criteria: **"F"** for **Gender.**
4. Criteria: **"F"** for **Gender, "Swimming"** for **MostDesiredFacility.**
5. Criteria: **"Football"** or **"Cricket"** for **MostDesiredFacility** ("Cricket" could also be on the Or line.)
6. Criteria: **"F"** for **Gender, <15** for **Age, "Indoors"** for **MostDesiredFacility.**
7. Uncheck the box in the **Show** line.
8. See figure.

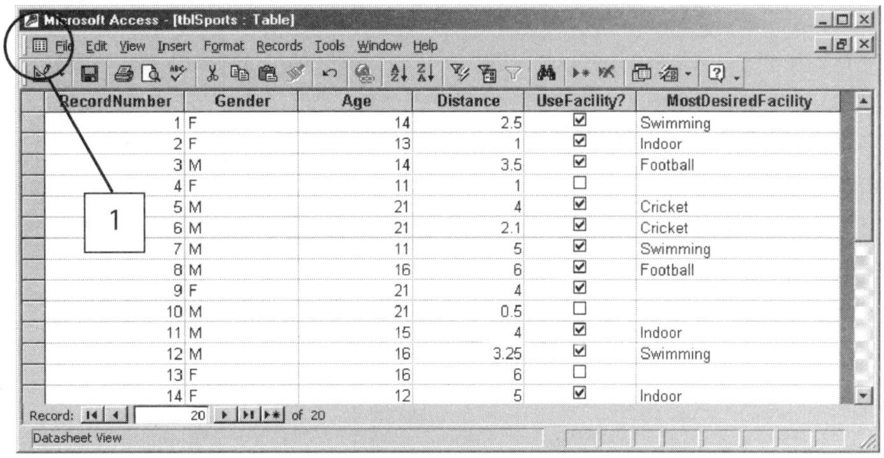

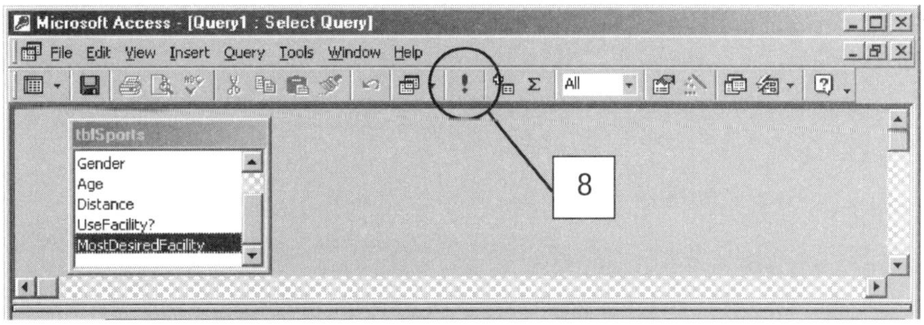

Sheet 6b Making Queries

1. 100.
2. **Age, UseFacility, Distance.**
3. The query.
4. See figure.
5. Criteria: **<4** for **Distance.**
6. Criteria: **<4** for **Distance, >= 14** for **Age** (or **> 13**).
7. Or: **"F"** for **Gender.**
8. Criteria: **"M"** for **Gender** , **Between 5 And 10** for **Distance, Yes** for **UseFacility.**

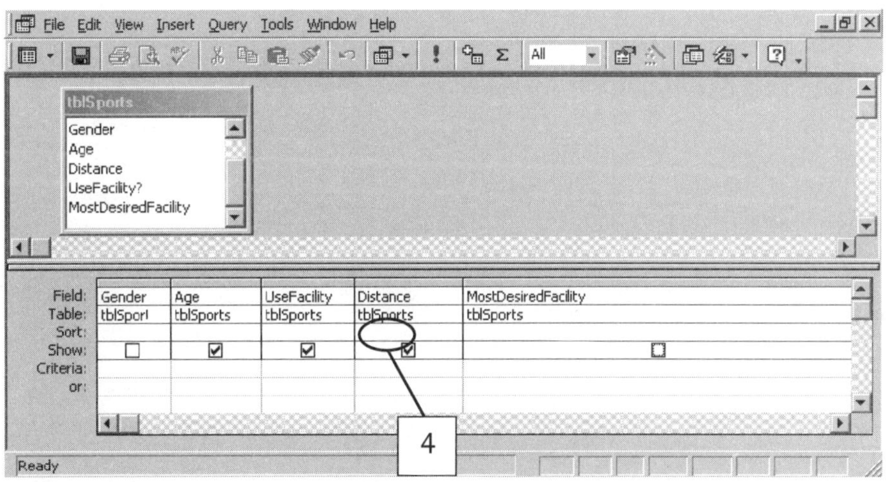

Sheet 7a Presenting Data

1. Click in the **tblSports** title, then click in it again until a text cursor appears; edit the title.
2. The date and page number.
3. The field values.
4. Select the label and field and drag the handles to resize them.
5. c) Pie chart
6. 25%
7. See figure.
8. Bar chart or column chart.

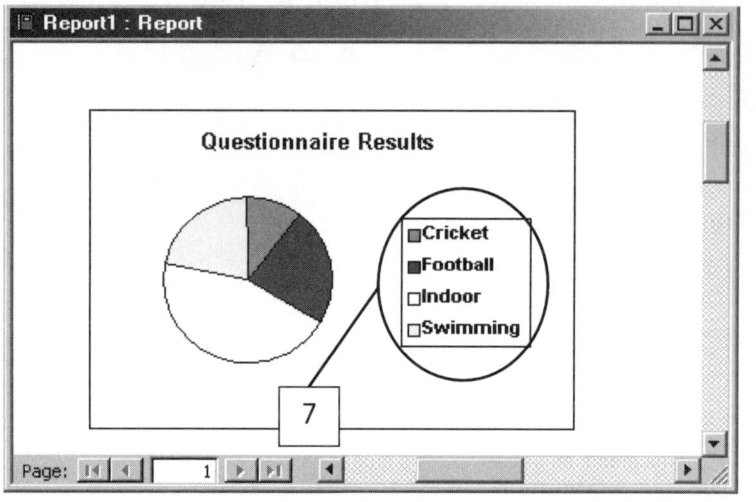

Sheet 7b Presenting Data

1. Make a query, setting criteria for **Date Last Serviced** to **< 01/04/2000**. Then base the report on this query.
2. **Date Last Serviced** (or Make and Model).
3. See figure.
4. See figure.
5. iii) Reports
6. Column chart.
7. No.
8. Number of cars, by Model.

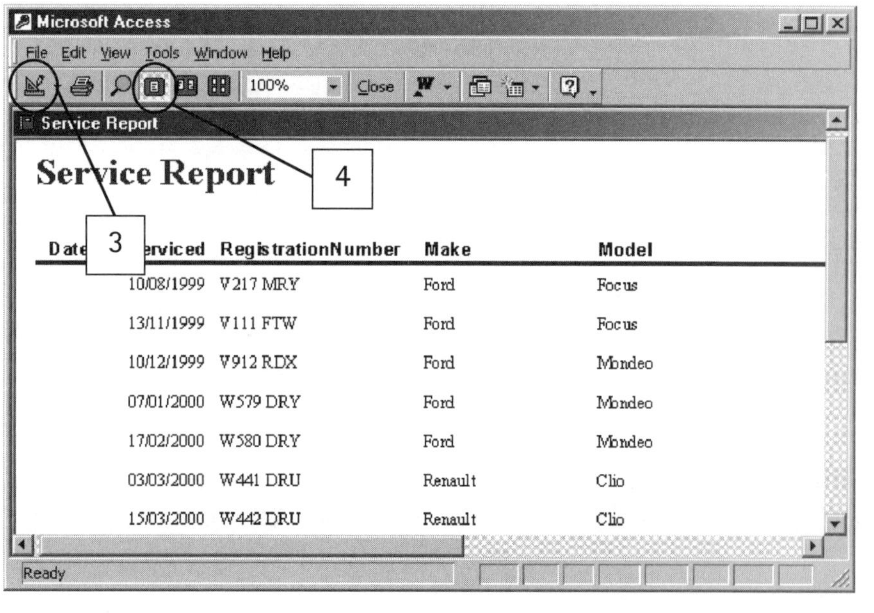

Sheet 8a Forms for Data Entry

1. Combo box.
2. Quick, easier than typing, less chance of making a mistake.
3. The tab order.
4. See figure.
5. Select the field, move the pointer over it until it becomes a hand, then drag it.
6. Select the field then drag the centre right handle inwards. (The pointer must be a double-headed arrow.)
7. See figure.
8. See figure.

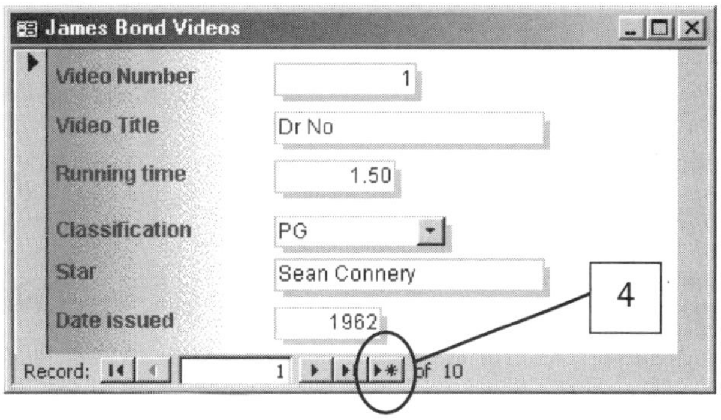

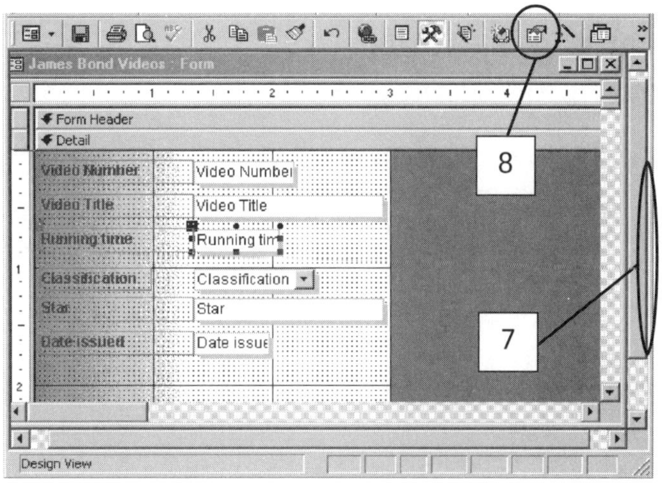

Sheet 8b Forms for Data Entry

1. Click the **First Record** navigation button (labelled 1 in figure).
2. See figure.
3. Click in the **Gender** field, click the **Find** button and enter **F**.
4. See figure.
5. Click the **Delete Record** button (labelled 5).
6. Click in the label and drag one of the side centre handles inwards. (The pointer must be a double-headed arrow.)
7. **MostDesiredFacility** or Gender
8. See figure.
9. See figure.
10. "M" or "F"

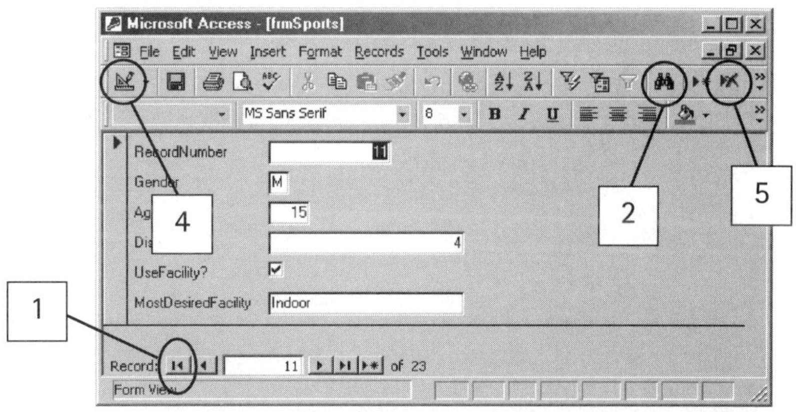

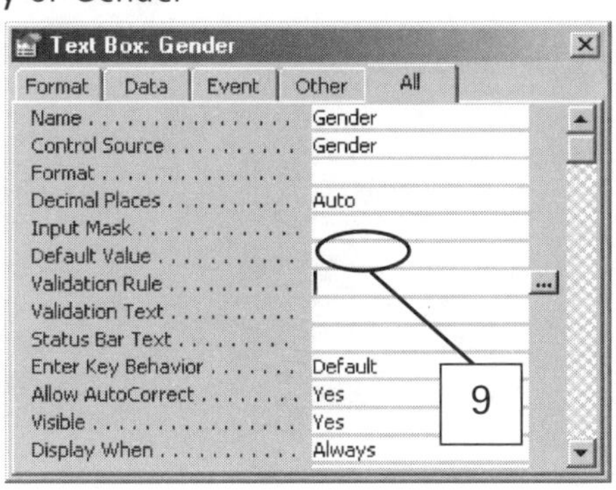

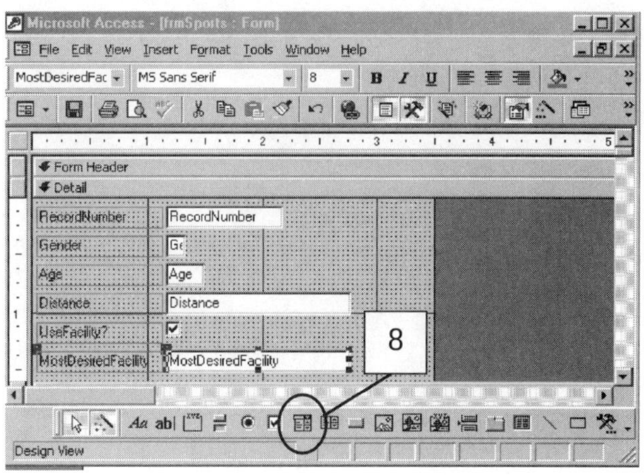

Record Sheet

Name: ______________________________ Class: __________

	Sheet	Date Completed	Teacher Initials
1. Introduction to Databases	1a:		
	1b:		
2. Creating a New Database	2a:		
	2b:		
3. Datasheet View	3a:		
	3b:		
4. Data Validation	4a:		
	4b:		
5. Formatting and Printing	5a:		
	5b:		
6. Making Queries	6a:		
	6b:		
7. Presenting Data	7a:		
	7b:		
8. Forms for Data Entry	8a:		
	8b:		

Certificate of Achievement

This is to certify that

has successfully completed

Basic Access 2000

Notes

Notes

Notes